the

honey

handbook

the honey handbook

andrea nasi

ilaria rattazzi

franz rivetti

Everest House
Publishers   New York

contents

the honey handbook

what is honey?

HONEY is produced from the nectar of flowers or from other sweet liquids that worker bees eat during each day's flying, which is finally stored in the cells of the beehives. Actually, there are more than 10,000 varieties of bees, but only 5 perform this act of honey storage. It has been calculated that to obtain one pound of honey, bees have to visit at least one million flowers. A honeybee lives four to six weeks and can collect only a teaspoonful of nectar. Since obviously many thousands of bees are employed to collect nectar and others in the hive must fan it with their wings to solidify it into honey, evaporating it by three-fourths, about 150,000 bees are required to produce one pound of honey. The flying distances involved in accumulating the nectar for that one pound are equivalent to flying three times around the earth.

Honey is made not only from flowers but also from certain herbaceous stalks and from leaves and grasses; we will be looking more closely at the sources of honey all over the world. Of the trifold origin of honey—leaves and twigs, branches and tree trunks, and flowers—the last leads to what we call real honey. The first is honeysweet or honeydew, and the second is named manna. In the United States honey usually comes from clover and alfalfa, but there are scores of exotic American honeys such as those from the tulip tree, spearmint, dandelion, raspberry, sagebrush, willow, and heartsease and is found from Maine to Florida swamps to Oregon to Arizona to Hawaii.

The widest known use of honey is clearly in various areas of gastronomy. Apart from uses as sweetener or preservative, its basic contributions as a food are through a range of health-promoting properties, which we will explore, and through its energetic power: a pound of honey supplies approximately sixteen hundred calories and therefore is equal to three pounds of beef, three and a half pounds of fish, five and a half pounds of milk, or twenty-five eggs. Equally important are the roles honey plays in medicine and veterinary medicine and in industry (cosmetics, leather tanning, tobacco, wines, drinks, and syrups) .

beekeeping through the centuries

HONEY has been known throughout recorded history; the ancients used to consider it a gift of Providence. Its use actually goes back to prehistory. In different parts of the Old World men learned to exploit the bee, searching for its treasured product in crevices and empty trunks of trees and putting it into the gradually more sophisticated beehives born with the beginning of apiculture, or, more commonly, beekeeping. A natural product of such high value could not be bypassed by a hungry marauder like man: right from the beginning he understood that this precious concentration of the sun's rays was worth a few stings from the robbed bees.

Honey and beeswax have been appreciated down through the ages; these products have been traded for thousands of years and praised with songs and poems throughout the centuries. Greek philosophers, fascinated by the fragrance of honey, believed it was a dew distilled from the stars and rainbows and thus an elixir of youth. As a potent source of energy, honey was given in substantial quantities to athletes competing in the early Olympic games. It was also said that it had aphrodisiac properties, and therefore honey was considered the number one component of all elixirs of love. In Ovid's list of his era's aphrodisiacs we find "honey on Hymettus flowing."

For many thousands of years, until the discovery of the New World and sugarcane, the only sweetener that man had was honey, the unique and precious food eaten by the gods of Olympus, the celestial gift praised in the Bible and the Koran, the beneficial drug prescribed by Hippocrates, Celsus, and Galen. It is impossible to recount all the ways honey was used in history. In this book we will try to show how modern science, even after rejecting many foolish fancies and explaining away a number of questionable legends, has proved that honey is no less interesting and useful than it appeared to be to Aristotle.

We begin with a chronological survey:

15,000 B.C.   The oldest depiction of man in the act of stealing honey from bees goes back to this period. It is a drawing of the Magdalenian (Paleolithic) period, found on a rock in the Queves of Arana near Valencia (Spain) . The picture shows two men climbing long sedge-grass ropes to a small shelter on a cliff. One of the pair is shown at the moment of digging out the honeycomb, putting it into a small basket, while bees fly all around.

3000 B.C.   Written memoirs tell us how beekeeping along the Nile River was a common occupation in ancient Egypt. Since warm weather came earlier in northern Egypt than in the south, the beemasters moved their bees along the Nile by following the flowering season. From the First Pharaonic Dynasty (3200–2780 B.C.) to the Roman period, the official documents of Egyptian kings always incorporated the symbol of the bee. The cartouche containing the name of the king was preceded by a bee and the same drawing could be found also in the tombs of the First Dynasty.

2050–1950 B.C.   In Assyria, during and after the reign of Sargon I, the bodies of the dead were treated with wax and buried in honey.

1580–1350 B.C.   A mural fresco of the Eighteenth Theban Dynasty in Egypt records a man carrying some honeycombs and grapes: a swarm of bees flies over the honeycombs. The color and shape of the bees are identical to the ones common nowadays.

1300 B.C.   In China, where the bee classified *Apis cerana* was found (as in India and Japan), writings refer to honey.

986–933 B.C.   King Solomon mentions honey and honeycombs in many writings. "My son, eat thou honey, because it is good; and the honeycomb, which is sweet to thy taste" (Proverbs 24:13).

640–599 B.C.   Solon, an Athenian legislator, ruled that no new beehive could be less than three hundred yards away from already existing ones.

400 B.C.   Xenophon, the Greek historian, describes the activities of the queen bee, comparing them to those of a housewife. He is the first to consider the queen as ruler of the beehive.

384–322 B.C.   Aristotle was the first to scientifically study bees. His writings contain observations recognized as accurate by modern science. He was the first to deny the theory of the spontaneous generation of the bee. He also noticed that during their flights, bees limit themselves to only one kind of flower. His works were the main source of information through the Middle Ages.

116–27 B.C.   Varro, erudite Roman author of some six hundred volumes, gives us considerable technical information about the beekeeping of that time. From his writings, it is obvious how beekeeping was already a commercial business in many countries surrounding the Mediterranean.

100 B.C.   According to Roman law, bees not enclosed in a beehive were legally considered without owner (*res nullius*). "Bees are wild by nature. For this reason, if you do not put up a beehive for the wild bees on a tree, they are—like the birds that make their nests in that tree—not to be considered yours. So that if somebody else gives them a home, he will become their owner."

70–19 B.C.   In Virgil's works we find profound affection and admiration for bees. He talks about them in the *Ecologues*, in the *Georgics*, and in the *Aeneid*. Virgil was a poet and a beemaster; his practical information and his instructions about maintaining beehives are very useful even though they do not have the scientific method of Aristotle. According to him, thyme honey is superior.

A.D. 800–900.   It is believed that bees were taken to America by the Irish and Norwegians. Between the ninth and tenth centuries, these peoples established a number of small colonies all the way to Narragansett Bay. Here they also built a mission, and as honey was at that time the only sweetener, and as beeswax was used in Catholic ceremonies, it is most likely that they had brought their bees with them.

1448–82.   During the Inca reign, Tupac Yupanqui conquered some territories whose inhabitants were formerly forest dwellers. This population was so poor that the only tribute they could pay was in the form of monkeys, parrots, honey, and wax (probably wild beeswax). This is the real beginning of the history of honey and bees in the New World.

1788.   Ernst Spilzer noted that when the bee goes back to its beehive with nectar, it makes certain movements—now known as "the dance of the bees."

In the eighteenth century, the use of honey was steadily diminishing and it almost disappeared in the modern era.

How is it possible, that after having been for thousands of years a reigning sweetener and one of the most precious foods, honey could experience a decline of this kind? The reason is that in the eighteenth century it was discovered that a much cheaper product could be obtained from sugarcane. During the Middle Ages, all proper manor houses kept beehives, but they and the manors themselves largely disappeared during the religious wars and later Renaissance era growth of urban society. From 1600 to 1900 little honey was available. Sugarcane had been brought to Europe in the eighth century by the Moors but was not widely used until honey had itself become the rare, luxurious substance.

And so in the eighteenth century the era of sugar began. Following the laws of industrial growth, more and more sugar was being produced because consumers were looking for something cheaper than honey and with roughly the same qualities. They did not know of course that this new white sweetener made only from saccharose had none of the precious elements, vitamins, minerals, and nutritive value of honey and that its unbalanced composition would help introduce—according to some of the most recent studies—what we may now call "civilization diseases."

honey as a cure

HONEY is very important in the therapeutic field, and we will, without trying to cover subjects that would be out of place in a book of this general nature, mention just a few of the ways in which it can be used to restore and improve health.

There is a considerable amount of literature about honey in medicine. Sometimes in combination with other drugs, it is used to treat a number of different ailments. Modern studies have confirmed the traditional belief that honey is an effective remedy for a cough and other illnesses of the respiratory system. They also verify that honey is helpful in pediatrics, in curing some digestive disorders (gastric ulcer or liver problems, particularly), in therapy for angina pectoris and myocardium infarction. It is good for the urinary tract, it fights anemia, it has antibacterial and laxative properties, and it promotes healing of wounds. It is, further, very important in cases of inflammation, in local applications, and for bedsores. It is often used in pharmacopoeia, as a sweetener and flavoring in the preparation of various medicines. Let us now briefly examine its effects on some organs of the human body.

Honey in Pediatric Medicine

It has been observed that assimilation of calcium and magnesium, vital elements for the forming of the skeleton, improves by giving milk with honey to children. Good results were obtained by using honey instead of other sweeteners in prepared baby formulas. Infants who have difficulty in digesting saccharose can digest perfectly the sugars present in honey. More important, it is used to cure children's constsipation, improves the functions of the gastroenteric organs, gives greater resistance to infectious diseases, and improves and encourages growth. Lastly it is helpful in calming the pain of teething.

Effect on the Respiratory System

It is known that honey melted in a warm liquid aids the emission of perspiration; it is thus a good cure of colds, bronchial catarrhs, and cough, through its significant expectorant property. It contains a natural antibiotic of the inibine group, and for this reason too it is used to fight many respiratory ailments.

Effect on the Circulatory System

Therapeutic use of honey indeed contributes to irrigation of cardiac muscles and blood vessels, moderates irregular cardiac activity, and has other immeasurable effects.

Antianemic and Reconstituent Effect

Various writers have noted that honey gives a good antianemic action due to a recently revealed factor. The dark honeys are especially rich in mineral salts (iron and magnesium in particular) , and these help in cases of debilitation, exhaustion, asthenia, and lack of appetite.

Action on the Digestive System

Honey has a beneficial and stimulating action on the digestive system. A protracted use of this product was considered to be useful in stomach diseases such as gastric ulcer, the progression of which was diminished and sometimes arrested. Honey, used alone or in a solution before and after meals, regulates the secretory and motive activity, improves the digestive and the intestinal reabsorption, and fosters easy elimination of the toxic substances from the liver.

Action on the Urinary Tract

The use of honey for curing a number of ailments of the urinary apparatus (nephritis, cystitis, and pyelitis) stems from its ability to facilitate the elimination of toxic substances. It is very useful for nephritic patients especially because it does not have albumin and it contains very little salt.

Action on the Nervous System

A therapy based on honey has a beneficial effect in some cases of neurosis, as it has mildly soporific action; it also increases one's capacity for work and it can work as an analgesic, soothing headaches and pain caused by arthritis.

Action on the Skin

Honey has been used in the treatment of furunculosis, and if it is blended with rye flour helps to aid the softening of hard abscesses, furuncles or boils, and inflamed swelling of the lymph glands. It also asssists the curing of aphthas when used a few times a day melted in lemon juice.

Honey in Traumatology and Surgery

In the time of the Egyptians, of Hippocrates, and during the Middle Ages, honey was already being used to cure wounds and burns, because of its anti-bacterial and chemical-physical properties.

During World War II, for example, this kind of medication was widely used in Russian hospitals with good results.

Honey in Pharmacology

Honey is often used by a pharmacist in the preparation of syrups, hydromels (when fermented this combination of honey and water is called mead) , and other honey solutions needed to minimize the unpleasant taste of some medicinal substances.

Here are a few examples of honey's soothing and healthful powers:

Wine with Honey

> **1 glass dry wine**
> **1 tablespoon honey**

Melt honey with 2 tablespoons wine. Add it to the rest of the wine and drink it very cold. It is energy-giving, stimulating, and a tonic.

Milk and Honey with Rum

1 cup hot milk
2 tablespoons honey
2 tablespoons rum

Combine all ingredients and blend until honey is well melted. Drink it hot. It is excellent in cases of cold and flu.

Hydromels

1 quart water
1¼ cups honey of lime
1 teaspoon lime ptisan

Put all ingredients in a saucepan and bring to a boil. Let cool, filter, and drink a little bit of it in the evening. This drink is good for insomnia, nervousness, and headache.

Spicy Tea

1⅓ quarts water
1 cinnamon stick
½ teaspoon cloves
3 teaspoons tea
2 teaspoons lemon juice
½ cup honey

Boil water with cinnamon and cloves over a low flame for 10 minutes and pour it on the tea in a teapot. Let it stand for a while. Filter and add lemon juice and honey. It is a fantastic pick-me-up.

why honey?

LITTLE by little we are starting to really appreciate honey—no longer considering it merely as another way to add flavor to cookies and loaves, along with butter and preserves. Only a few of us nevertheless are learning to understand that honey is really a food, and fewer still know that it is even more than that; it is rather a complete and complex group of foods.

In order to better understand the importance of honey, it is necessary to know something about sugars. Not sugar as we usually know it, but those sugars that appear in chemistry textbooks as complicated patterns of lines and symbols. Never fear: We are not asking you to dig out those dusty school books—because the job sugar does in keeping our bodies going is as simple as it is basic.

Carbohydrates, a basic and irreplaceable source of energy, have to be digested before they can be utilized by the body. Of course this takes some time and, therefore, the actual intake of energy is delayed, compared to when they were introduced into our body. Some carbohydrates, however, do not need to be processed by the intestines and thus supply the body with almost instant energy. These carbohydrates are sugars of various kinds and can be divided into two groups: the mono-saccharides (or simple sugars) and the polysaccharides (or complex sugars), the second ones being combinations of the first. Before arriving in the bloodstream, the complex sugars have to be changed into simple sugars, and this can take place only with the help of digestion. From the nutritional point of view, the two simple sugars of greatest importance are saccharose (sugarcane or beet sugar) and the lactose that constitutes almost 40 percent of the solid substances of milk. The saccharose, before being utilized, has to be processed and divided into the two simple sugars that are present in it: dextrose and levulose. Simple sugars do not require such a complicated procedure but are available in nature only in some fruits and in honey. In this last instance, the digestive process is simplified by the fact that the bees have already processed the complex sugars found on flowers. Since honey is made of many kinds of sugars, its energetic value is among the highest to be found in natural products. What does actually happen when we eat a tablespoon of honey? The dextrose and the levulose are immediately asssimilated, while the other sugars present in small quantities have to be digested slowly, therefore constituting a further storage of fuel for the body.

As we have seen, then, honey is a remarkable source of energy, but its qualities do not end here. For all the other elements present in it, however small the quantities, contribute to its unique biological/physiological value. Specifically, dextrose and levulose make up roughly 75 percent, water 17.2 percent, and the balance is composed of different kinds of sugars, as well as aromatic substances, proteins, minerals (calcium, sodium, iron, phosphorus, etc.), vitamins, organic acids, enzymes, antibiotics, and a small amount of still unknown elements.

Because of its antibacterial content, honey can be considered hygienically safe and this has been proven in laboratory tests, where it was contaminated with germs of some of the most serious diseases. These germs were destroyed by honey in a matter of hours. Once more, though, we want to stress the fact that the most important quality of honey is what has been very accurately described as a "marvelous biological mosaic," in other words, a system of interacting elements for which honey, perhaps more than any other substance, can be called a truly "living food."

Honey and Athletes

Once again, the basic elements of honey are dextrose, which can be immediately utilized by the body, and levulose, normally stored by the liver, which will release it to the organism. Among the other elements of honey one in particular was recently discovered: it is called glikutile and apparently helps the absorption of sugars in the muscular tissues.

When one knows of the role of glikutile, it is easy to understand how important honey is for athletes. It has been demonstrated, for example, that a few tablespoons of honey taken before a protracted physical effort increases the resistance of the athlete. If taken after the effort, it will help to quickly restore energy. It is a good habit for anyone who has to exercise and study in the same general time frame to eat some honey after the physical effort in order to eliminate promptly the symptoms of fatigue and resume other activity in the optimal physical and psychological condition.

Honey used during intervals of soccer or other particularly tiring sports helps athletes not to resent the stress too much and make it more easily through the last minutes of the game. For those who have two or more stressing athletic events in the same day, honey is beneficial between one and the other, for it restores quickly the spent energy. During protracted events, honey in sufficient quantity (approximately half a pound during the day) avoids the excessive weight losses caused by perspiring and energy consumption. If you are instead trying to lose some weight, honey can be equally useful if eaten at the end of a light meal because it helps to reduce appetite and will make you feel replete, restoring at the same time the energy you may be lacking because of the moderate food intake.

Honey and Children

Kids may be greedy in some ways, but their principal greediness is only the need to eat, during those vital growing years, foods with a high energy content. Children's greediness is in fact particularly aimed at sweets—chocolate, candies, and so on—and it is of course precisely these sweets that contain the largest amounts of sugar, and that is, as we have seen, the nutrient with the highest capability to supply energy. This in itself would not be too serious, but as a practical matter it happens that many of these foods can be hard to digest because of their composition and especially because of the complex processing which is a part of their manufacture.

How many times have we said to our children that chocolate is bad for your liver, that sugar and candy are bad for your teeth, that you must not eat too many sweets, and that greediness, in other words, is a bad habit? A general habit of eating excessive quantities of sweets and similar things is harmful. But what we will normally notice in our kids is a physiological need, and as such we must respect it: fulfill it when it is true necessity, fight it when it tends to become just a bad habit.

Many times we ask ourselves how children can keep moving and jumping around all day long. We know all too well that for us half that exercise would impel us to stay in bed for a week before we could even speak again. In fact, putting their simple locomotion aside, if we consider the amount of energy required by those little active bodies, needing more and more fuel to multiply their cells and grow, we must admit that this need of energetic food is amply justified.

If we examine the characteristics of honey, we must come to the conclusion that it should have first place in a scale of priorities not only among sweets but also among foods in general. Honey supplies almost instant energy, and this feature is accompanied by other advantages, by no means less important. Let us examine them in detail.

Many children do not digest white sugar easily, but they have no such problems with honey, which we have learned has been predigested by the bees and can therefore be promptly utilized by the organism. Some scientists even believe that the levulose of honey is more easily digested than lactose (the sugar found in milk).

Since honey's sugars do not have to be modified during the digestive process, they do not cause any intestinal fermentation. If we mix the children's food with honey, their digestion will be smoother and their appetite will improve. Honey given in the right quantity and to an empty stomach is helpful for intestinal peristalsis. It is a good laxative that, even taken in high quantities, does not cause diarrhea or other troubles of this kind.

Some kinds of honey and in particular

the aromatic ones contain certain substances that have a soothing effect. Given
small quantities of them, children fall
asleep very easily. Some scientists have
shown that honey helps the absorption of
both calcium and magnesium at once.
During the years of growth, such minerals
are particularly significant for the bone
structure. Honey also has the very
important quality of great appeal to
children. A slice of buttered bread with
honey will seldom be refused. Honey
melted in milk is a delicious drink and
blended with cream cheese will probably
receive a standing ovation from your
youngsters. And last but not least, it is
good just as it is, in spoonfuls, according
to the most established techniques of
childhood robbery, especially if you were
clever enough to hide the jar but not too
well, to store it in a high place but not too
high, thus allowing them the fun of that
little act of piracy.

honeys of the world

THE NUMEROUS honeys that exist are characterized by their color, aroma, thickness and granulation, and, of course, taste. Depending on which flowers honey is made from, its color varies from white to dark, almost black. Honey made from the nectar of evergreens is blond, the one made from acacias is light yellow, green is the honey from heather and lime, that from chestnut and ivy is quite dark, that from clover and rosemary is pale (the famous French rosemary honey is granular and white), and amber with red tones is the honey from orange blossoms. There is black honey found in Brazil, and in North Carolina it is possible to find "blue honey," the origin of which is not yet known. Almost all honeys are fluorescent; that is, they emit light of various colors when exposed to ultraviolet rays.

Thickness and granulation—the process of crystallization—depends on the contents of fructose. You can buy honey in either comb or "extracted" form, the latter being either liquid or crystallized. Crystallized honey may be a spread or called creamed or candied. Sometimes honey is pasteurized to prevent crystallization, but then it is not as nutritious.

The scent is due to the very light

aromatic substances of the flowers. Some honeys have a strong perfume (those from lavender, thyme, lime, acacia) , some others such as those from the sainfoin **plant** or lucerne (alfalfa) , both native to Eurasia, have only a very weak aroma. There are sweet or less sweet honeys, some more or less sharp to the tongue, others more or less bitter. Some trees can give honey an unpleasant taste; usually very dark honey is extremely strong in taste. The sweetest honeys are those from rosemary, orange, and lavender; the most bitter comes from wormwood.

Honey has the same curative characteristics of the tree or of the flowers from which it originates. It should be noted that not all honey from a particular type of plant will have exactly the same qualities; they are affected by different climate, soil, etc. One may nevertheless classify types of honey, as follows:

Acacia honey. Energetic, detoxicating, and capable of supplying minerals. Some experts judge Hungarian acacia honey as the finest in the world.

Cabbage honey. This is indicated for respiratory ailments.

Conifer honey. Suggested for bronchitis.

Eucalyptus honey. Fights the cough caused by tracheitis or bronchitis and urinary tract infections.

Hawthorn honey. Fights cardiac diseases, calms the nervous system, and is suggested in the cure of arteriosclerosis and dyspepsia.

Heather honey. Diuretic and anti-rheumatic. It is used for urinary diseases and as a reconstituent. Commonly found in the British Isles and northern Europe, these heather honeys soon became thick, or jellylike.

Lime honey. Used as a sedative. It is suggested for insomnia, headache, and in some cases of arteriosclerosis.

Orange honey. A good sedative and, therefore, suggested for insomnia.

Rosemary honey. Suggested for liver ailments and for sore throat. It is a good energetic in cases of asthenia and during convalescence.

Thyme honey. This type is very good against bronchitis and common cold. It is especially suggested in cases of asthenia and lack of appetite. This was the honey used by the Greeks and is perhaps the oldest known form.

Still other sources include coffee plant, dogwood, buckwheat, black locust, anise, and countless others.

honey for personal beauty

It comes as a surprise to many that honey is used in the manufacture of cosmetics. But this is true, through the roles played by three important qualities of the substance:

1. *It holds humidity* and is capable of maintaining or replenishing the correct amount of moisture in one's skin.

2. *It is an acidic* substance and therefore helps eliminate acne, blackheads, and all sorts of irritations.

3. *It is a tonic;* it makes the complexion smoother and younger looking by reducing wrinkles and restoring natural elasticity to the skin.

Try to use the mask most suitable to your skin type regularly. In a short period of time, your face will regain its clear radiance and the skin will be once again soft.

Mask for Acne

    1 tablespoon honey
    1 tablespoon cooked peaches, puréed

Blend honey and peaches thoroughly. Wash face with hot water and spread mask lightly over face with fingertips. After 15 minutes rinse with hot and then cold water.

Moisturizing Lotion

    2 tablespoons honey
    2 tablespoons skim milk

Heat honey with milk and pour into jar. Massage face and neck gently with cotton pad soaked in lotion. Rinse with warm water.

Honey Mask

Dip fingers in honey and spread it over previously washed face and neck. Massage with a slow, upward circular motion. Then start tapping lightly with fingertips until they begin to stick to the skin. After 20 minutes rinse with warm and then cold water.

Honey Soap

    4 ounces plain bath soap
    1 tablespoon water
    1¼ cups honey

Cut soap in thin slices and boil for a few minutes in a pan with water and honey. Add a few drops of your favorite perfume. Pour into a mold and allow to harden. If you use this soap regularly, your skin will be smooth and velvetlike.

Honey Compress I

    ½ cup bran
    1 tablespoon honey
    5 tablespoons rose water

Mix bran, honey, and rose water together and work into a soft paste (if necessary, add more rose water). Spread generously over previously washed face and neck. After 30 minutes rinse with a sponge dipped in warm water.
ACTION: cleanses and softens skin.

Honey Compress II

   ½ cup fresh almonds
   ½ cup honey

Grind almonds very fine and blend with honey to make a thick, smooth paste. Spread over previously washed face and neck, avoiding eyes and lips. After 30 minutes, rinse with sponge dipped in warm water.
ACTION: makes skin soft and velvety.

Mask for Dry Skin I

> 1 egg yolk
> 1 tablespoon milk
> ½ teaspoon honey
> 1 teaspoon powdered milk

Beat yolk and add other ingredients, mixing thoroughly. Spread mask over face and neck. After 15 minutes rinse with warm and then cold water.

Mask for Dry Skin II

> 1 tablespoon honey
> 1 tablespoon sweet almond oil
> 1 tablespoon rose water

Blend all ingredients and spread over previously washed face and neck. After 15 minutes rinse with warm and then cold water.
ACTION: moisturizes skin and eliminates wrinkles.

Mask for Dry Skin III

> 1 tablespoon sweet almond oil
> 2 tablespoons honey

Proceed as in previous recipes, but leave on skin for 30 minutes.

Mask for Oily Skin

> 1 tablespoon honey
> 1 tablespoon lemon juice
> 2–3 drops milk

Mix honey in lemon juice and add enough milk to obtain a smooth paste. Spread on previously washed face and neck. After 10–15 minutes rinse with a sponge dipped in warm water. Do not use more than once every 2 weeks or once a month, if your skin dries up too much.

Youth Mask

> 1 tablespoon honey
> 1 tablespoon flour
> a few drops rose water

Blend ingredients into a smooth paste. Spread over previously washed face and neck. After 30 minutes rinse with a sponge dipped in cold water. Use this mask twice a week.

Lotion for Freckles

1¼ cups honey
¼ cup glycerin
¼ cup rubbing alcohol
½ teaspoon citric acid
15 drops ambergris

Blend all ingredients thoroughly and apply lotion with cotton, in morning and before bedtime.

Hand Cream

8 egg yolks
2 cups honey
2 cups almond oil
½ pound bitter almonds, finely minced
½ teaspoon oil of orange

Beat egg yolks with honey, add almond oil gradually, and then almonds and oil of orange. Apply small amount to hands to maintain a youthful appearance.

Lotion for Chapped Hands

½ cup honey
½ cup glycerin
Few drops tincture of benzoin
3 tablespoons rose water

Pour all ingredients in a bottle and shake until they are perfectly blended. Spread lotion on hands at bedtime and wear a pair of gloves to bed.

Hair Lotion

1 teaspoon honey
¼ cup eau de cologne (your favorite brand)
½ cup olive oil

Mix honey and cologne thoroughly. Then add oil and mix again. Massage head with lotion 30 minutes before washing your hair. Shampoo hair twice.
ACTION: prevents hair loss and dandruff.

in the kitchen

EVERYBODY knows that honey is more expensive than sugar. When one suggests the use of honey, one is compelled to give some pretty convincing reasons. First of all, honey's chemical properties are more wholesome and nutritious than that of sugar. Honey is also hygroscopic: it has the quality of absorbing and holding moisture. For this reason, bread and pies of all kinds will remain tender and fresh longer when made with honey than when sweetened only with sugar. Honey is used as a nourishment for the leaven in preparing bread or dough. It makes food not only sweeter but also more savory.

The sweetening quality of honey is similar to that of sugar. You can, we find, substitute it in every recipe and in every other preparation by using the amount indicated for sugar. Others feel honey is actually sweeter and reduce the amount. It's a matter of taste.

Here are a few hints to enable you to use honey properly, satisfactorily, and easily:

It needs to be kept at room temperature.

To melt a thick or granulous honey, it is necessary to dip the jar in warm water until the honey is liquefied.

It is difficult to determine the weight of honey. The best solution is to weigh the full jar and take out the honey that you need. For example, if the jar weighs 20 ounces and, according to your recipe, you need only 4 ounces of it, you will take out honey until the jar will weigh 16 ounces. It is sometimes useful to know that 3½ ounces of honey are equal to 4 full tablespoons.

By greasing a tablespoon with some oil or butter, it will be easier to measure out and handle honey. When you replace sugar with honey in a recipe, you would decrease the amount of liquid or butter (reduce liquid or butter by roughly 1/5 of measurement of honey) . This procedure is not necessary in baking bread or cakes with chocolate, dates, raisins, walnuts, and dried fruit.

For breaking down the acidity of honey,

it is better to add to the flour a pinch of baking soda (½ teaspoon every 12 ounces).

The oven temperature has to be low to moderate (300–350°). Since honey candies at a lower temperature than sugar does, it may caramelize if the oven is set too high.

Before removing bread or cakes from baking tins, it is better to let them cool off for a while.

If you want to keep bread or cake for some time, wrap them in aluminum foil. If you want to preserve the freshness of cookies, put them in a tin box or glass jar and seal them hermetically. After a few days they will taste even better. If bread becomes dry and stale, roll it up in a wet cloth, put it into a plastic bag, and keep it in the refrigerator for 12 hours. After this time, take the bag and cloth off, wrap the bread in aluminum foil, and warm it in the oven for a few minutes at 300°. It will again be soft and fresh.

When you use honey in cold sauces, always melt it with some liquid before adding it to other ingredients.

In the recipes that we will give you, you will notice that we often talk of the kneading trough. This machine is used a lot because it saves time. Especially when you use honey, this machine gives you a good homogeneous mixture and you do not need to get your hands messy.

When you make bread, use only clear honey, such as the one from acacia.

When you prepare honey ice cream, remember that honey needs a very low temperature to solidify. It will take longer to thicken but it will have a better aroma and delicious taste.

In some recipes we suggest a specific honey, but you are free to replace it with the one you prefer. Try different kinds so you can choose the ones you like best for particular purposes.

We always use honey instead of sugar in tea, coffee, milk for children, fresh or cooked fruit, cakes, cookies, candies, and preserves. The range of recipes offered now goes far beyond such obvious uses; it is our hope that they serve to increase your love of honey and especially to entice you to include honey often in your own cooking.

SAUCES AND DRESSINGS

Honey Ketchup

4 pounds tomatoes, peeled and
  chopped
3 medium onions, chopped
3 tablespoons honey
1 teaspoon Italian herbs
½ teaspoon cumin seeds
1 teaspoon powdered cloves
1 teaspoon black pepper
½ teaspoon powdered cinnamon
1 teaspoon dry mustard
½ teaspoon cayenne pepper
1 teaspoon salt
½ cup red wine vinegar

Cook tomatoes and onions over low heat
for about 15 minutes. Add honey, herbs,
and spices and cook until the sauce
thickens. Blend and add vinegar. Allow to
cool, pour in a tightly covered glass jar,
and preserve in refrigerator.

Tomato Sauce for Pasta

1 pound tomatoes, peeled and
  chopped
¼ cup olive oil
1 teaspoon salt
1 teaspoon honey
1 teaspoon dried basil or a handful
  fresh basil leaves
1 teaspoon thyme
½ teaspoon black pepper

Cook all ingredients over low heat for 15
minutes. Strain and then return to pot and
bring to a boil. Immediately pour over
freshly cooked spaghetti.

Honey Sauce for Duck

4 tablespoons butter
¾ cup honey
⅓ cup chopped almonds

Warm blended ingredients and pour over
roasted duck.

Mint Sauce for Roast Lamb

¼ cup beef bouillon
1 tablespoon vinegar
1¼ cups honey
Handful fresh mint leaves
3 tablespoons dried mint

Heat bouillon and vinegar in a pan. Add honey, mix well, and add fresh and dried mint. Boil over low heat for 5 minutes. Use as a marinade before cooking or as a separate sauce.

Salad Dressing

¼ cup olive oil
½ cup lemon juice
½ cup honey
1 teaspoon salt
1 teaspoon oregano
1 teaspoon rosemary
1 teaspoon thyme
½ tablespoon sweet paprika

Blend all ingredients. Can be refrigerated in a glass jar up to 6 months.

VEGETABLES

Honeyed Beets

3 cups grated raw beets
4 leaves fresh basil
1 bay leaf
¼ cup water
Salt to taste
2 teaspoons honey
½ cup yogurt

Place beets, basil, bay leaf in water and boil over low heat for 5 minutes. Remove laurel, add salt, honey, and yogurt. Serve hot or cold.

Sweet and Sour Cabbage

½ red cabbage, chopped
Juice of 2 lemons
3 tablespoons honey
2 tablespoons olive oil
3 medium onions, chopped
½ cup beef bouillon
1 tablespoon cumin seeds
½ cup golden raisins
Pinch mixed herbs
1 tablespoon soy sauce

Combine all ingredients in pot, cover, and boil over low heat for 15 minutes. Can be served hot or cold.

Russian Cabbage Borscht

2 medium onions, chopped
1 clove garlic
10 medium tomatoes, chopped
5 potatoes (unpeeled), thinly sliced
2 small cabbages, very thinly sliced
1 bay leaf
1 teaspoon thyme
Salt to taste
Cayenne pepper to taste
¾ cup plus 2 tablespoons honey
Juice of 1½ lemons

Fill a large pot halfway with water and simmer onions and garlic for a few minutes. Add tomatoes, potatoes, cabbage, bay leaf, and thyme. Cover and cook over low heat for 1 hour. Add salt, pepper, honey, and lemon juice and cook 30 minutes more. Serve very hot with toasted white bread.

French Peas

1-ounce package frozen peas
4 tablespoons plus 1 teaspoon butter
1 head iceberg lettuce, chopped
1 tablespoon parsley
1 tablespoon thyme
1 teaspoon honey
Salt and pepper to taste

Put peas in 1 cup boiling water. As soon as the water returns to a boil, drain and set aside. Melt 4 tablespoons butter in a pan, add lettuce, thyme, honey, parsley, salt, pepper, and a few tablespoons of water. Cover and cook for 5 minutes. Add peas and cook 10 minutes more over very low heat. Add 1 teaspoon of butter, allow to melt, and serve.

Luello Carrots

2 pounds carrots
8 tablespoons butter
1 teaspoon honey
Salt to taste
¼ cup brandy
1 tablespoon fresh minced parsley

Pare carrots and cut in thick slices. Melt butter in a frying pan, add carrots, honey, and salt. Cover with a sheet of waxed paper and lid and cook over low heat for 10 minutes. When carrots are almost ready, add brandy and cook 10 minutes more. Add parsley and serve.

Braised Baby Onions

18 pearl onions, peeled
¼ cup chicken bouillon
¼ cup white vinegar
12 tablespoons butter
2 tablespoons honey
Salt to taste

Marinate onions with bouillon and vinegar for six hours. Drain and reserve liquid. Melt butter in a pan, add onions, and brown on all sides. Add honey and allow it to caramelize, lightly shaking pan. Add reserved bouillon, cover, and cook over low heat until the onions are tender. Salt to taste and serve very hot.

Sweet and Sour Cucumbers

4 cucumbers
2 tablespoons olive oil
½ cup yogurt
3 tablespoons vinegar
1 tablespoon powdered dill
2 tablespoon honey

Peel cucumbers, slice, and cover with large-grain sea salt, to eliminate excess water. After 1 hour rinse slices in cold water and blot with paper towel. Blend oil, yogurt, vinegar, dill, and honey and pour over cucumbers. Chill for 30 minutes before serving.

Sweet and Sour String Beans

½ cup olive oil
2 tablespoons vinegar
1 teaspoon tarragon
1 tablespoon honey
1 tablespoon sauce
1 pound string beans, salted and
   steamed for 8–10 minutes

Blend oil, vinegar, tarragon, honey, and soy sauce and pour over string beans. Allow to rest 15 minutes before serving. Serve at room temperature.

MEAT

Honey Lamb

    7 ounces dried apricots
    2 medium onions, chopped
    4 tablespoons butter
    Salt and pepper to taste
    2 tablespoons curry powder
    3 tablespoons red wine vinegar
    10 tablespoons honey
    4 tablespoons dry white wine
    2 pounds (approximately) lamb
        shoulder, cut in small cubes

Cook apricots in a little water, pulverize in processor, and blend with the juice. Sauté onions with butter in a pan. Add apricots, salt, pepper, curry powder, vinegar, and honey and cook over low heat for 10 minutes. Add wine and mix thoroughly. Pour sauce over meat and marinate for 12 hours. Drain meat, divide between 6 skewers, and broil 2 inches from flame, rotating skewers so meat cooks evenly. For medium rare, broil 10 minutes; for well done, 15 minutes. Serve very hot with heated marinade.

Orange Duck

    1 3-pound (approximately) duck
    3 tablespoons butter
    Salt and pepper to taste
    4 oranges
    ¼ cup honey
    Juice of 1 lemon
    2 tablespoons vinegar

Brown duck with butter in a pan. Add salt and pepper, cover, and cook over moderate heat for 45 minutes, basting from time to time with the liquid. Peel 2 oranges, cut peel in thin strips, cook 2 minutes in boiling water, and drain. In a small pan, boil over moderate heat honey, juice from 2 remaining oranges, lemon juice, vinegar, and orange peel, and add cooking liquid of duck. Cut duck, cover with thin slices of 2 peeled oranges, and pour sauce over it.

Honey Pigeons

    1 teaspoon salt
    2 pigeons
    2 tablespoons honey
    1 cup soybean oil
    1 tablespoon soy sauce

Spread salt in interior of pigeons and honey on exterior. Fry in very hot oil for 20 minutes. Drain, cut, and serve with soy sauce dribbled over each pigeon.

Ginger Chicken

4 tablespoons butter
2 tablespoons minced onions
1 teaspoon salt
1 teaspoon ginger
2 tablespoons lemon juice
6 tablespoons honey
½ cup orange or apple juice
2 teaspoons soy sauce
1 3-pound chicken

Combine all ingredients except chicken in pan and cook over low heat for 5 minutes. Marinate chicken in sauce for 12 hours. Bake chicken in oven at 350° for 20 minutes. Turn chicken upside down, cover with half the ginger sauce, and bake at 300° for 20 minutes. Turn around again, add remaining sauce, and leave in hot oven for another few minutes. Serve with boiled rice.

Orange Roasted Pork

1 3–4-pound pork roast
Salt and pepper to taste
3 tablespoons honey
1 orange
½ chicken bouillon cube

Tie roast, sprinkle with salt and pepper, and roast in oven with a little water at 350° for 1 hour. Brush with honey and cook 30 minutes more. Grate orange peel and squeeze juice from orange. Take roast out of pan and keep warm. Remove fat from cooking pan to the remaining cooking juices and add the peel and juice of orange. Melt bouillon cube with a few tablespoons water and add to sauce. Cook over low heat for a few minutes. Slice roast, cover with orange sauce, and serve.

Baked Ham

1 small ham (10 pounds)
1¼ cups honey
4 teaspoons dry mustard
2 teaspoons arrowroot
20 cloves
2 cups dry white wine or pineapple juice

Put ham in pan and bake in oven at 325° for 1¼ hours. Remove skin and fat from surface. Dilute honey, mustard, and arrowroot with a few spoons of cooking sauce and spread over ham. Insert cloves and pour wine or pineapple juice over ham. Bake in oven at 425° for 30 minutes adding more sauce frequently. Cut in thin slices and serve. It will keep well and it is delicious served cold.

Orange Ham

1 ½-inch-thick ham slice
½ cup honey
1 cup orange juice
½ teaspoon powdered cloves
½ teaspoon tarragon

Place ham slice in a broiling pan. Melt honey and orange juice in a pan, add cloves and tarragon, and pour over ham. Cover with a sheet of aluminum foil and bake in oven at 325° for 1 hour and 15 minutes. Remove foil and roast 15 minutes more.

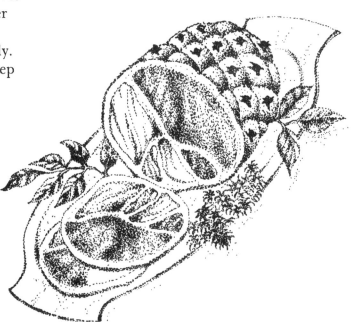

Honey Pork Rib

    1 tablespoon thyme
    1 tablespoon savory
    ¼ cup honey
    1 cup dry white wine
    3½ pounds pork rib
    Salt and pepper to taste
    2 cloves
    ½ teaspoon sweet paprika

Blend the thyme, savory, honey and wine. Place pork in a deep pan and pour the mixture over it. Season with salt, pepper, cloves, and paprika. Cover and cook in oven at 350° until tender. Add a few tablespoons of wine. Serve very hot with sliced apples.

Pork Polonaise

    2 tablespoons honey
    Salt and pepper to taste
    6 1½-inch-thick pork chops
    1 small head cabbage
    ½ teaspoon cumin seeds
    1 large onion, thinly sliced
    1 cup heavy cream
    ½ cup grated Swiss cheese

Spread honey, salt, and pepper on both sides of chops. Split cabbage in eight sections and cover with boiling water. Simmer for 10 minutes, drain, and put in large buttered pan. Sprinkle with cumin seeds. Add onion and pork. Heat cream and add Swiss cheese. Remove from fire and mix until cheese is melted. Pour over chops. Cook in oven at 350° for 45 minutes.

Glazed Pork Fillet

    3½ pounds pork fillet
    ¼ cup dry white wine
    1 teaspoon powdered ginger
    1 cup honey
    8 tablespoons soy sauce

Marinate pork in wine and ginger for 12 hours. Drain and dry with paper towels. Cook in oven at 425° for 2 hours. Brush once in a while with honey melted in soy sauce. Serve with fried or boiled rice.

FRUIT AND NUTS

Almond Milk

    3 tablespoons peeled almonds
    2 teaspoons honey
    1¼ cups water

Combine ingredients in blender until perfectly blended.

Pignolia Milk

    3 tablespoons pignolias (pine nuts)
    2 tablespoons honey
    1¼ cups water

Combine ingredients in blender until perfectly blended.

Apricot Shake

    7 ounces dried apricots
    2 tablespoons honey
    1 cup yogurt

Rinse apricots, cover with water, and store in cool place for 12 hours. Blend the apricots with honey, add yogurt, mix, chill, and serve.

Date Shake

    1 cup yogurt
    1 cup milk
    4 ice cubes
    12 dates, pitted
    3 tablespoons honey
    4 almonds

Blend all ingredients thoroughly. Chill and serve.

Amber Sauce

    1 cup yogurt
    2 tablespoons honey

Mix and store in refrigerator. Serve with raspberries, grapes, strawberries, and peaches.

Red Wine Sauce

1 cup red wine
½ cup plus 2 tablespoons orange
   juice
7 tablespoons honey
½ teaspoon cinnamon
1 tablespoon cornstarch
1 clove

Blend all ingredients except clove
thoroughly. Add clove and cook over
moderate heat, stirring with a wooden
spoon. When sauce is thick and smooth,
remove clove. This sauce is very good with
crêpes or croquettes.

Honey Sauce

7 tablespoons honey
2–3 tablespoons lemon juice
¼ teaspoon paprika

Blend all ingredients. Delicious as a
topping for oranges, grapefruit, and all
berries.

Fruit Salad Sauce

¼ cup yogurt
2 teaspoons raisins
1 tablespoon chopped walnuts
1 tablespoon grated coconut
3 tablespoons honey
1 tablespoon lemon juice

Blend all ingredients. Store in refrigerator.
Delicious with pears, apples, and bananas.

Muesli

1 tablespoon oat flakes
3 tablespoons water
3 tablespoons yogurt
1 teaspoon lemon juice
1 teaspoon honey
1 apple, grated
1 tablespoon minced walnuts,
   almonds, and hazelnuts

Soak oat flakes in water. Blend yogurt,
lemon juice, and honey and add to oat
flakes. Add apple (with peel) and sprinkle
with minced nuts.

Carrot and Orange Salad

> 4 grated carrots
> ¼ cup raisins
> 2 oranges, sliced
> ½ cup yogurt
> 3 tablespoons honey

Combine carrots, raisins, and oranges and dress with yogurt and honey.

Tropical Salad

> 2 tablespoons honey
> 1 teaspoon lemon juice
> 1 cup yogurt
> 3 apples, grated
> ½ cup minced dates
> ½ cup minced walnuts
> Grated coconut

Melt honey with lemon juice, add yogurt, apples, dates, and walnuts. Sprinkle with grated coconut and serve.

Syruped Grapes

> ½ pound white grapes
> ½ pound red grapes
> ¼ cup honey
> 1 teaspoon lemon juice
> 2 tablespoons sherry
> 1 tablespoon toasted slivered almonds

Cut grapes in half and remove the pits. Melt honey with lemon juice and sherry. Place the grapes in a bowl, then add the honey mixture. Marinate for 2 hours at room temperature, then refrigerate. Serve in individual bowls and decorate with almonds.

Melons with Wine

> 1 tablespoon mint leaves
> 1 tablespoon grated lemon peel
> ½ teaspoon powdered cardamom
> 1 tablespoon honey
> ¼ teaspoon salt
> ¾ cup dry white wine
> ¼ cup lemon juice
> 1 cup honey dew melon balls
> 1 cup cantaloupe melon balls

Mash together mint leaves and lemon peel with cardamom, honey, and salt. Add wine and lemon juice. Soak until the honey is all melted. Place melon balls in a glass or ceramic bowl, add the mixture, and refrigerate for 2 hours before serving.

Baked Grapefruit

> 4 grapefruit
> ½ cup honey
> 6 tablespoons sherry

Cut grapefruit in halves, remove the sections, and place on a cookie sheet lined with aluminum foil. Melt honey and sherry and spoon over the sections. Bake at 400° for 20 minutes. Serve hot.

Pears with Wine

> 1½ pounds pears
> 2 4 oz. glasses red wine (e.g., Barolo)
> 1½ cups honey
> 1 clove
> 1 cinnamon stick
> 1 cup raisins, soaked for 2 hours in
>   ½ glass of wine

Peel pears without removing the stem. Place upright in a pan, add the wine, honey, clove, and cinnamon, and cook over low heat for 20 minutes. Add raisins and its juice and cook for another 20 minutes. The pears must be soft but not mushy. Serve at once.

Strawberries with Cointreau

> 1 pound strawberries
> ¼ cup honey
> 1 cup heavy cream
> 4 tablespoons Cointreau

Wash strawberries, cover with honey, and refrigerate for 3 hours. Whip cream, add Cointreau, and spoon on top of the strawberries.

Figs with Honey

8 figs
Juice of 1 lemon
1 tablespoon thick honey
Pinch of grated nutmeg

Peel and halve figs. Place lemon juice and honey in a pan, bring to a boil, add the figs and nutmeg, and cook for a few minutes. Pour in a bowl, let cool, then refrigerate for at least 2 hours. Serve with whipped cream or yogurt.

Walnuts with Honey

1 cup sugar
½ teaspoon salt
½ cup honey
⅓ cup water
1 vanilla bean
⅔ pound walnut meats

Place sugar, salt, honey, water, and vanilla in a pan. Bring to a boil and cook for 5 minutes. Remove the vanilla. Add walnuts, mix rapidly, then pour the mixture over greased marble or aluminum foil. Spread the mixture well with a spatula. Cool for 1 hour, then cut into serving portions.

Bananas au Rhum

6 bananas
4 tablespoons butter
½ cup honey
1 tablespoon cinnamon
3 tablespoons rum

Peel bananas, cut in half lengthwise, and sauté in butter. Place the slices in a baking dish. Blend the honey, cinnamon, and rum over low heat, pour over the bananas, and bake at 400° for 3 minutes. Serve hot.

Flambé Peaches and Strawberries

4 peaches
2 cups water
½ cup honey
1 lemon peel
¼ stick cinnamon
½ pound strawberries
1 teaspoon grated orange peel
¼ cup cognac

Place peaches in a pan and cover with water and honey. Add lemon peel and cinnamon and boil for 15 minutes. Drain. Set aside ⅓ cup of the syrup. Peel the peaches, cut in half, remove the pit, and place cut side down in a baking dish. Mash the strawberries with the grated orange peel and the syrup. Pour this mixture over the peaches. Place in the oven and bake at 350° for 10 minutes. Heat cognac in a small pan, pour over the peaches, and ignite. Serve immediately with whipped cream or a fruit ice cream.

Fruit Ka-Bob

½ cup honey
3 tablespoons lemon juice
4 tablespoons butter
2 apples
2 pears
1 small cantaloupe

Place honey, lemon juice, and butter in a pan. Heat over low heat, mixing all the time, until melted and well blended. Wash the fruits, but do not remove the peel. Cut in sections and place in the honey mixture. Place the sections on skewers and broil or bake at 400,° brushing occasionally with the sauce, until the mixture is crusty.

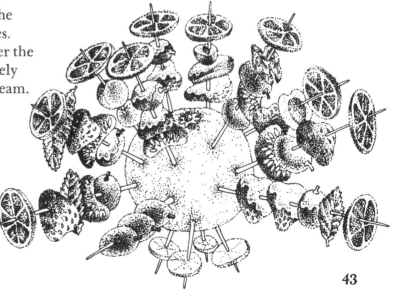

43

Fried Apples with Honey and Rum

½ cup honey
⅓ cup dark rum
Juice and grated peel of ½ lemon
1 pound apples
1 cup flour plus flour for dredging
1 pinch salt
⅓ cup lukewarm water
5 tablespoons oil
2 egg whites
1 cup heavy cream

Heat honey. When completely melted remove from flame and add rum, lemon juice, and lemon peel. Peel and core apples and cut into ½" rings. Place in a bowl, pour the honey over them, and let sit for 1 hour, mixing occasionally. Sift 1 cup flour and salt, then mix with water and 1 tablespoon oil until smooth. Let rest for 1 hour. Beat egg whites until stiff and add to the batter. Drain the apples, setting aside the syrup. Dredge the apples in flour, heat ¼ cup oil in a skillet, dip the apple rings in the batter, and fry until crisp and golden. Drain and place on paper towels. Whip the cream, mix with the remaining honey syrup, and pour over the fried apples. Serve at once.

Baked Apples with Honey

4 apples
1 teaspoon butter
½ cup honey
1 cup heavy cream
1 pinch cinnamon

Peel and core apples and cut into ½" rings. Spread butter on one side and place in a large baking dish buttered side down. Pour honey over and bake for 8 minutes. Whip cream and cinnamon and serve with the apples.

Blackberries Kissel

1 pound blackberries
3 tablespoons honey
Juice and grated peel of ½ lemon
1 pinch grated nutmeg
1 teaspoon whole wheat flour

Wash blackberries, place in a pan with honey, lemon juice, nutmeg, and enough water to cover. Cook for 20 minutes, until soft, then mash. Dilute flour with a few spoonfuls of mashed blackberries, add to the blackberry mixture, and cook until thick. Pour in a glass bowl or in individual bowls and refrigerate for a few hours. Decorate with grated lemon peel.
NOTE: Blueberries may be substituted.

Baked Bananas with Orange

  4 large bananas
  1 teaspoon butter
  4 oranges
  6 tablespoons orange honey
  1 pinch cinnamon

Peel bananas, cut in half lengthwise, and place in a buttered baking dish. Peel 2 oranges, remove the membrane, cut in slices, and place over the bananas. Squeeze the other 2 oranges and add honey and cinnamon to the juice. Mix well, pour over the orange slices, and bake at 350° for 20 minutes.

Winter Fruit Salad

  1 banana
  1 pear
  1 apple
  6 dates, pitted
  6 tablespoons honey
  Juice of 2 tangerines
  4 tablespoons ground walnuts

Peel and cube banana and pear. Cut apple in cubes. Cut dates in small pieces. Melt honey in tangerine juice and place in a bowl with fruit. Let stand for 1 hour. Sprinkle with ground walnuts before serving.

Mint Sauce for Fruit Salad

  1 bunch fresh mint
  1 tablespoon honey
  2 tablespoons lemon juice
  16 ounces (2 containers) yogurt

Chop the mint and mix with the honey and lemon juice. Add to the yogurt and refrigerate for 1 hour before using.

Summer's Dream

½ pound raspberries
½ pound blackberries
¼ pound black currants
½ cup honey
12 slices slightly stale white bread
2 cups whipped cream (optional)

Place fruits and honey in a saucepan, boil for 1 minute, then let cool. Remove crusts from bread slices and line the bottom and sides of a baking dish with some of the bread. Pour the fruits in it, setting aside some of the juice, and cover with more bread slices. Press well and weight with a slightly smaller dish. Refrigerate for 12 hours, then unmold into a high-sided serving dish. Serve with the juice previously set aside, and, if you wish, whipped cream.

Kierciel

1 teaspoon cornstarch
1½ cups fruit juice (the one you prefer)
2–3 tablespoons honey
1 teaspoon green chartreuse, cointreau, or other liqueur
1 cup sour cream

Mix cornstarch with half the fruit juice, then add the rest of the juice and the honey. Cook over very low heat, mixing constantly, until the mixture is thick. Coat the inside of a round ring mold with liqueur and pour in the mixture. Let cool, then refrigerate for at least 6 hours. Unmold and serve with sour cream and cookies of your choice.

Baked Apples with Honey

4 apples
1 teaspoon butter
¼ cup honey
Juice of 1 lemon
3 ounces raisins (soaked in warm water
    for 1 hour)
1 teaspoon allspice

Core apples and place in a buttered baking dish. Blend together honey, lemon juice, raisins, and allspice and fill the centers of the apples with this mixture. Bake at 350° for 50 minutes.

Basic Honey Fruit Sauce

⅓ cup orange juice
Juice of 1 lemon
3 tablespoons honey
Pinch of cinnamon
Pinch of nutmeg

Blend together all ingredients and pour over fruit (drained and cut in large pieces).

BREADS

Brown Honey Bread   Makes 2 loaves

- 1 cup honey
- 2 cups warm milk
- 1½ cups warm water
- 2 ounces yeast
- ¼ cup oil
- 1 tablespoon salt
- 3½ pounds whole wheat flour

Mix honey with milk and water. Add yeast and set aside for 5 minutes. Add oil, salt, and half the flour and knead for 10 minutes. Gradually add remaining flour and knead for 5 minutes. Put the dough in a greased bowl, cover it, and allow to rise in a warm, draft-free place for about 1 hour. Knead again until flat and allow to rise again. Press, knead quickly, and divide in half. Place in 10″ x 4″ x 3″ loaf pans and bake in oven at 350° for 1 hour. Brush surface with honey while they are still hot.

Sweet Bread

- ½ cup honey
- ½ cup water
- 1 pinch baking soda
- ½ teaspoon salt
- ¼ cup melted butter
- 2 cups flour, sifted

Mix honey, water, baking soda, salt, and melted butter together in a blender. Add sifted flour to the mixture and blend again until smooth. Pour into a rectangular mold lined with aluminum foil and bake at 350° for 40 minutes. Do not open the oven while the bread is baking.

Honey Oat Bread — Makes 2 loaves

2 ounces yeast
1 quart warm milk
1 pound oats
1 teaspoon salt
¾ cup honey
¼ cup oil
7–8 cups flour

Dissolve yeast in ½ cup of warm milk. Pour oats, salt, honey, oil, and yeast into the remaining milk and mix well. Gradually add the flour, mixing well. Knead the dough for 10 minutes. Then cover with a clean towel and allow to rise. Press it down and allow once more to rise. Place on a floured surface and knead for 10 minutes more. Divide the dough in half and place in greased bread pans. Cover with a towel and allow to rise until volume is doubled. Place the molds in a baking pan in which you will have poured some hot water and bake in oven at 325° for 1½ hours.

Limpa (Swedish Rye Bread) — Makes 2 loaves

2 ounces yeast
1 cup warm milk
3 tablespoons honey
1 tablespoon salt
1 tablespoon baking powder
1 tablespoon powdered anise
1 tablespoon powdered cumin
2 cups chicken bouillon
2½ pounds rye flour
Grated peel of 2 oranges
3 tablespoons vegetable oil

Dissolve yeast in warm milk. Add all other ingredients and mix well. Knead for 5 minutes. Place the dough in a greased bowl, cover, and let it rise in a warm, draft-free place for 1 hour. Divide the dough in half, shape it into 2 rounds, and let it rise again for 30 minutes. Bake on a flat sheet at 325° for 1 hour.

Walnut Sweet Bread

½ cup sugar
¾ cup honey
8 tablespoons butter
4 cups flour
1 teaspoon baking soda
1 egg
1 teaspoon salt
¾ cup milk
1⅓ cups crushed walnuts

Cream sugar and butter. Add egg, flour, yeast, baking soda and salt and mix well. Blend milk, honey and walnuts and fold them through the mixture. Pour the batter into a greased and floured loaf pan and bake at 350° for 1 hour.

Anise Bread

1 tablespoon anise seeds
2 cups water
2 tablespoons honey
18 ounces flour
1 teaspoon baking soda

Boil anise in water for 2 minutes. Remove from fire and allow to rest 15 minutes, then strain. Add honey, bring to a boil, then pour over flour and baking soda and mix. Pour into a baking pan lined with greased aluminum foil and cover with a flat pan. Place a weight on it and bake in oven at 325° for 2½ hours.

Spicy Spanish Bread

1 cup sugar
1 cup honey
2 teaspoons baking soda
1 teaspoon powdered anise seed
½ teaspoon powdered cinnamon
2 tablespoons thyme
18 ounces sifted flour
1 cup water

Melt in a pan sugar, honey, and baking soda. Remove from fire and add anise, cinnamon and thyme. Then little by little add the flour. Mix with a wooden spoon until the paste is homogeneous, adding water as needed. Pour into 2 round 10″ square baking pans lined with greased aluminum foil. Bake for 5 minutes at 400°, then lower heat to 350° and bake for 1 hour.

Betz Bread

⅓ cup crushed walnuts
⅓ cup peeled and crushed almonds
⅓ cup raisins, soaked in warm water for 30 minutes and drained
1 pinch salt
1 pinch pepper
1 pinch nutmeg
2 ounces fondant chocolate cut in small pieces
2 ounces candied fruit, cut in small pieces
½ cup honey

Combine in a bowl all ingredients except honey and flour. Melt ¼ cup honey with 2 tablespoons water and add to other ingredients. Add enough sifted flour to obtain a dough soft and elastic. Shape it in small rolls and place in a baking pan lined with greased aluminum foil. Brush surface with remaining honey and cook in oven at 400° until brown.

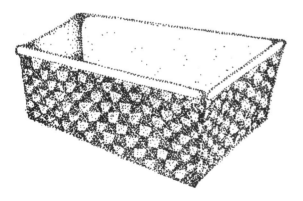

Tyrolean Zelten

1½ pounds chopped dried figs
⅓ cup raisins, soaked for 30 minutes in warm water and drained
½ pound chopped dates
1 cup chopped candied orange
1 cup chopped candied pineapple
¼ pound crushed walnuts
¼ pound whole wheat paste
½ cup rum
½ cup brandy
1 pinch powdered cinnamon
1 pinch salt

Place in a large mixing bowl figs, raisins, dates, orange, pineapple, walnuts, cinnamon, and salt. Pour liquors over it and allow to rest for 15 minutes. Add whole wheat paste and mix until well-blended. Shape in small oval loaves, sprinkle with some candied fruit, and place in a rectangular baking pan lined with greased aluminum foil. Bake in oven at 350° for 15 minutes. Brush with honey while still hot. Can be preserved for several weeks if wrapped in aluminum foil.

Indian Pudding

1½ quarts milk
12 ounces corn meal
1 pound honey
1¼ cups sugar
4 tablespoons butter
1 teaspoon salt
1½ tablespoons powdered cinnamon
½ teaspoon powdered nutmeg
½ teaspoon baking soda
¼ pound dates

Simmer milk and flour in a large saucepan for 20 minutes. Add other ingredients, mix well, and pour into a rectangular baking pan 12″ long and lined with foil. Cook at 325° for 2 hours. Serve hot with a chocolate sauce or with ice cream.

Honey Date Cake

1 pound dates
Flour
½ cup honey
1 teaspoon baking soda
1 pinch salt
½ cup milk
½ cup water

Pit and mash dates. Add all remaining ingredients and mix well. Pour the mixture into a greased loaf pan and bake at 350° for about 45 minutes. The blade of a knife will come out clean if the cake is ready.

Honey Cake

8 tablespoons butter
1 cup cane sugar
4 eggs, separated
2 cups flour
1 teaspoon baking powder
½ cup honey
Pinch of baking soda
1 tablespoon milk

Mix thoroughly butter and sugar. Add honey and egg yolks and keep mixing. Next add flour, baking powder, and baking soda, carefully sifted, and the whipped egg whites. Pour in a 15-inch long baking pan lined with aluminum foil and bake at 375° for 40 minutes. Allow to cool before removing from pan.

Coffee and Honey Cake

14 ounces sifted flour
2 teaspoons baking powder
¾ teaspoon baking soda
¾ teaspoon salt
¼ teaspoon ginger
½ teaspoon powdered cloves
½ teaspoon allspice
4 tablespoons butter
1 cup sugar
2 eggs
½ cup honey
Grated peel of 1 lemon
½ cup strong coffee
⅓ cup raisins
⅓ crushed walnuts

Beat butter with sugar until soft and foamy. Add eggs 1 at a time, always mixing, and then honey and lemon peel. Add coffee, alternating with flour, baking powder, baking soda, salt, ginger, cloves, and allspice, and keep mixing. At the end, add raisins and walnuts. Pour into a 10″ long baking pan lined with greased aluminum foil and cut through it several times with a knife to eliminate air bubbles. Bake in oven at 350° for 45 minutes. Allow to cool before removing from oven. Wrapped in aluminum foil, it can be preserved for several weeks.

PIES, CAKES, AND COOKIES

Honey Butter

>   ½ pound honey
>   16 tablespoons butter

Blend ingredients thoroughly in blender and use as filling for cakes or as a spread. Can be refrigerated for 2 weeks.

Cocoa Syrup

>   1½ cups honey
>   1 pinch salt
>   ¼ pound sifted cocoa
>   ½ pint water
>   1 vanilla bean

Blend water, salt, and cocoa in a food processor. Pour into a saucepan. Add honey and vanilla and boil for 3 minutes, mixing constantly. Remove vanilla bean and allow to cool. Serve with cakes or ice cream. Preserve in refrigerator in a glass jar.

Honey Topping

>   1 egg white
>   ¼ pound honey

Beat egg white until foamy. Gradually add honey, mixing until it thickens. Use as topping for cakes and puddings.

Honey Chocolate Sauce

>   ¼ fondant chocolate
>   1 cup honey
>   4 ounces Grand Marnier
>   1 teaspoon butter
>   1 pinch salt
>   Grated peel of 1 orange

Combine all ingredients and simmer, constantly stirring, until perfectly blended. Allow to cool and serve with vanilla ice cream or cake.

Honey Glaze

2 ounces butter
12 ounces confectioner's sugar
½ cup honey
3 tablespoons hot milk

Beat butter and sugar with a wooden spoon, then add honey slowly, mixing continually, then add enough milk to form a clear, smooth paste.

Chocolate Glaze

2 ounces bitter fondant chocolate
2½ ounces heavy cream
1½ ounces honey
2 ounces sugar

Melt sugar in a small pot with two tablespoons water, add chocolate in small pieces, honey, and cream. Cook, always stirring, for 5 minutes. Use as icing for cake or with ice cream.

Cinnamon Honey Butter

¼ pound butter
½ cup honey
1 teaspoon powdered cinnamon

Mix all ingredients with a wooden spoon until well-blended. Serve with crêpes or spread on toast.

Honey Cream for Crêpes

4 tablespoons butter
½ cup honey
2 ounces heavy cream

Blend butter and honey in food processor. Add cream gradually and keep blending until soft and foamy. Serve with crêpes, hot puddings, and cakes.

Pâte Brisée (*pie crust dough*)
(Enough to line a 10-inch round pan)

3 cups flour
½ teaspoon salt
5 tablespoons butter at room
    temperature
3 tablespoons cold water

Blend all ingredients either by hand or in a blender. The dough must be smooth, if necessary add a little more water. Spread over a lightly floured surface and use in a 10-inch pie plate previously lined with buttered aluminum foil.

Pâte Sucré (*sweet pie crust dough*)
(Enough to line a 10-inch round pan)

3 cups flour
5 tablespoons butter at room
    temperature
1 cup sugar
3 egg yolks

Blend all ingredients rapidly either by hand or in a blender. The dough must be smooth, but do not overbeat. Spread over a lightly floured surface and use in a 10-inch pie plate previously lined with buttered aluminum foil.

Orange Cake

1 large orange, cubed (include the
    peel)
¼ pound raisins
¼ cup walnuts
3 cups flour
1 teaspoon baking powder
¼ teaspoon baking soda
1 teaspoon salt
1 cup honey
4 ounces butter
1 cup milk
2 eggs, beaten

Mix together the orange cubes, raisins, and walnuts and put aside. Mix all other ingredients either in a blender or by hand until smooth. Add the fruit mixture and mix until thoroughly blended. Pour the mixture into a 10-inch round pan, lined with aluminum foil and buttered. Bake at 350° for 45 minutes. Serve this cake with a honey cream or glaze.

Simple Honey Cake

1½ cups honey
8 ounces butter
1½ cups flour
5 tablespoons cornstarch
Grated peel of 1 lemon
8 egg yolks
5 egg whites

Mix the honey and butter in a blender until light and foamy. Add the lemon peel and the egg yolks and mix again. Sift the flour and cornstarch together and add. Beat the egg whites until stiff and fold lightly into the mixture. Pour into a 10-inch round pan, lined with buttered aluminum foil. Bake at 350° for 50 minutes.

Polenta and Walnut Cake

3 cups corn flour
8 ounces ground walnuts
¼ pound raisins (previously soaked in lukewarm water for 1 hour)
5 ounces butter
5 tablespoons acacia honey
4 eggs, separated
½ teaspoon baking powder
Pinch of baking soda
2 tablespoons lemon juice
Pinch of salt

Cream the butter in a blender or in a bowl with a wooden spoon. Beat egg yolks and add to the butter. Mix honey with the lemon juice and add to the egg and butter mixture. Then add the salt, baking powder, and baking soda (sifted together). Gradually add the corn flour, raisins (drained and dried), ground walnuts, and finally the egg whites, beaten until stiff. Pour the mixture in a buttered mold. Bake at 400° for 45 minutes. Remove from pan when cooled.

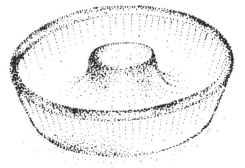

Carrot Cake

1 cup liquid acacia honey
7 eggs (separated)
8 ounces ground almonds
4 medium carrots, grated
1 teaspoon rum
1 pinch salt
1 teaspoon cinnamon

Beat the egg yolks and honey until light and foamy. Add the carrots, almonds, rum, salt, and cinnamon and mix well. Beat the egg whites until stiff and fold lightly into the mixture. Pour into a 12-inch round pan lined with buttered aluminum foil. Bake at 350° for 30 minutes. Remove when cool.

Cheese and Honey Cake

1 baked 8-inch pie crust
1 container plain yogurt
½ cup cream cheese
1 cup honey
Grated peel of 1 lemon

Blend together the yogurt, honey, and lemon peel until soft and foamy. Pour the mixture into the pie crust and refrigerate for 2 hours. Top with whipped cream or honey glaze.

Fez Cake (a Moroccan treat!)

1 cup honey
1 cup ground dates
½ cup toasted ground peanuts
4 eggs, separated
2 teaspoons cinnamon
1 tablespoon vanilla sugar
1 pinch saffron

Beat the egg whites until very stiff. Beat 3 egg yolks with the honey, add dates, peanuts, spices, and finally the egg whites. Pour the mixture into a 9-inch round pan, lined with buttered aluminum foil. Bake at 350° for 35 minutes. Remove from pan when cooled; serve with a honey cream.

St. Valentine's Apple Cake

1 8-inch baked pie crust
1 pound apples, peeled and cored
2 tablespoons water
2 ounces acacia honey
Grated peel of 1 lemon
1 cup flour
9 tablespoons butter
1 cup sugar
2 eggs
¼ cup ground almonds
Confectioner's sugar

Slice the apples and simmer them with the honey, a little bit of water, and the lemon peel over low heat. Remove when tender. Cool and mash them. Mix the sugar and butter, add the eggs, almonds, and finally the sifted flour. Pour the apples in the mold and pour the mixture over it. Roll out the remainder of the pie dough and cut into thin strips. Use them to decorate the cake. Bake at 350° for 30–40 minutes. Dust with confectioner's sugar and serve.

Fruit and Yogurt Pie

1 recipe Pâte Brisée (pie crust dough)
2 eggs
⅓ pound honey
¼ pound raisins
⅓ pound yogurt
½ teaspoon cinnamon
½ teaspoon nutmeg
⅓ pound pureed fresh fruits (prunes, apples, pears, peaches, or apricots)

Line a 9-inch round pan with aluminum foil and butter it. Spread in it half the amount of the pie dough. Beat the egg yolks with an electric blender, add the yogurt, then the pureed fruits, honey, raisins, and spices. Beat the egg whites until stiff, fold them lightly into the mixture, and pour in the pan. Cover completely with a thin layer of dough, sealing well at the edges. Bake at 350° for 50 minutes.

Raisin Pie

1 8-inch pie crust
1 teaspoon cornstarch
½ teaspoon salt
1 teaspoon cinnamon
¼ teaspoon ground cloves
¼ teaspoon ground nutmeg
Grated peel of 2 oranges
3 eggs, separated
6 tablespoons sugar
1 cup acacia honey
1 cup heavy cream
2 tablespoons heavy cream
⅔ cup golden raisins

Place the cornstarch, salt, spices, and the egg yolks in a double boiler and mix well. Add the honey, cream, raisins, and the grated orange peel. Cook at very low heat for 10 minutes, mixing constantly. When thickened, pour the mixture into the pie crust. Beat the egg whites until very stiff, gradually adding all of the sugar. Cover the mixture with the egg whites, particularly at the edges. Bake at 400° for 5–10 minutes, or until the egg whites are golden. Cool before serving.

Dried Fruit and Cream Pie

1 recipe Pâte Brisée (pie crust dough)
3 eggs
2¼ cups milk
⅓ pound ground, pitted dates (or prunes, raisins, or grated coconut)
1/6 pound honey
Pinch of salt
Grated nutmeg

Line a 10-inch pan with aluminum foil and butter it. Spread the dough in it. Beat together the eggs, milk, salt, and honey. Add the fruit and pour the mixture in the pan. Sprinkle with grated nutmeg and bake at 350° for 50 minutes. Remove from pan when cooled.

Hazelnut and Honey Cake

5 eggs, separated
½ cup acacia honey
¼ cup sifted flour
5 ounces ground hazelnuts
1½ tablespoons sugar
2 tablespoons heavy cream
1 tablespoon butter
Pinch of salt

Beat the egg yolks together with the honey, flour, hazelnuts, and sugar. Add the heavy cream and beat some more. Beat the egg whites until stiff and fold lightly into the mixture. Pour in a 10-inch round pan lined with buttered aluminum foil. Bake at 325° for 20 minutes. Remove from pan when still warm.

Honey and Chocolate Cake

    5 ounces semi-sweet chocolate
    ¼ pound butter
    ¾ cup honey
    2 whole eggs
    3 egg yolks
    3 ounces sifted flour
    Pinch sifted baking soda

Melt the chocolate and honey in a double boiler. Place the butter in a blender, pour the chocolate and honey over it, and mix until perfectly blended together (this can also be done by hand) . Add the eggs, one at a time, mixing constantly. Add the flour and baking soda and continue mixing until smooth. Pour in a 9-inch round pan lined with buttered aluminum foil. Bake at 350° for 25–30 minutes: the cake should be very soft inside.

Honey and Almond Cake

    4 ounces ground almonds
    2 ounces candied orange peel
    1 cup orange flower honey
    4 tablespoons cane sugar
    1 cup flour
    ½ cup sugar syrup
    1 teaspoon kirsch (cherry liqueur)
    1 teaspoon cinnamon
    ¼ teaspoon powdered clove
    Grated peel and juice of 1 lemon
    1 teaspoon yeast

Bring honey to a boil over low heat. Place the almonds, candied orange peel, sugar, kirsch, cinnamon, cloves, salt, juice, and grated lemon peel. In a blender, add the honey and blend well. Add the sifted flour and yeast and a few tablespoons of water. Mix until the dough is soft and even. Pour into a buttered 10-inch round pan. Bake at 400° for 20 minutes. Remove and soak with sugar syrup.

Raisin Cake

1 cup honey
1 tablespoon butter
1 egg, beaten
½ pound raisins
Pinch of powdered cloves
¾ cup water
2 cups flour
½ teaspoon baking soda
1 teaspoon cinnamon
Pinch of nutmeg

Place the raisins in a pan, cover with water, and bring to a boil. Boil for one minute. Keep ½ cup of raisin liquid on the side, cool the raisins. Beat the honey and butter until light and foamy, add the egg and then the flour, baking soda, and the sifted spices. Add the raisins and raisin liquid. Pour the mixture into a 9-inch round pan lined with buttered aluminum foil. Bake at 325° for 30 minutes. The cake must have a golden color. Serve with a honey cream or decorate it with a honey glaze.

Palermo's Pizzicata (recipe from Sicily)

4 cups flour
1½ cups honey
2 ounces candied citron rind, cubed
1 tablespoon sugar
Grated peel of 1 lemon
Grated peel of 1 orange
5 eggs
Pinch of salt
3 tablespoons butter (or shortening)

Mix (in a blender or by hand) the flour, sugar, lemon peel, salt, eggs, and butter. Work the dough into small balls and deep-fry in hot oil. Drain on paper. Heat the honey with the orange peel in a double boiler and pour over the balls. Place the balls on a serving dish and serve when cooled.

Certosino (recipe of the Certosa di Bologna monks)

1 cup flour, sifted
½ cup honey
½ cup sugar
4 ounces raisins
4 ounces shelled almonds
½ cup boiling water
4 ounces pine seeds
4 ounces ground candied citron
4 ounces grated semi-sweet chocolate
1 teaspoon baking soda
1 tablespoon anise seeds

Mix the honey, sugar, baking soda, and anise seeds in a bowl. Add the boiling water and mix well. Gradually add the sifted flour. Continue mixing and then add the raisins, almonds, citron, pine seeds, and chocolate. Pour the mixture into a 10-inch round cake pan, lined with buttered aluminum foil, and decorate the surface with some candied fruits. Bake at 375° for about 40 minutes or until golden. Can be kept for 2 months wrapped in aluminum foil.

Honey Clafoutis (recipe from France)

1 recipe Pâte Brisée (pie crust dough)
2 eggs
3 ounces acacia honey
2 ounces flour
½ cup milk
½ cup heavy cream
2 cups pitted cherries

Line a 10-inch round pan with buttered aluminum foil. Spread the dough in it pricking the bottom with a fork, and marking the edges. Place the cherries on the bottom. Beat together the eggs, flour, milk, heavy cream and honey. Strain the mixture and pour over the cherries. Bake at 350° for 40 minutes, or until golden brown. Serve either warm or cold with cream. The cherries can be replaced by the same quantity of prunes, apricots, peaches, or apples with raisins and walnuts.

Bestmors Kage (recipe from Denmark)

1 cup flour
1 cup rye flour
8 eggs
1¼ cups honey
1¼ cups sugar
1 tablespoon yeast
½ teaspoon pepper
½ teaspoon powdered cardamon
½ pound Malaga raisins
½ pound dried prunes, quartered
½ pound dry figs, quartered
4 ounces butter
½ teaspoon powdered cloves
2 teaspoons powdered cinnamon
¼ cup peeled almonds cut in half
    lengthwise
2 ounces candied oranges cut in cubes
2 ounces candied citron cut in cubes
1 teaspoon powdered ginger
Pinch of salt

Melt half the sugar in a pan, add the honey, and bring to a boil. Add the remainder of the sugar and the butter. Let this mixture cool, then add the yeast dissolved in 3 teaspoons of lukewarm milk. Beat and add the eggs, flour, the sifted spices, salt and candied fruits. Mix well, then add the almonds and the fruits. Pour the mixture in two loaf pans 8 inches long. Bake at 350° for 1½ hours (the cakes are done when an inserted toothpick comes out dry). Remove from pans when cooled. Can be kept for months wrapped in aluminum foil.

Honey Piquant Burbonnais (French Honey Cake)

2 cups flour
2 eggs
¼ pound melted butter
2 ounces acacia honey
½ teaspoon honey
1 cup warm water
1⅓ pounds apples, peeled and cut into cubes

Mix all ingredients, except the apples, well until the mixture is thick and even. Add the apples and mix with a wooden spoon. Pour the mixture into a loaf pan lined with buttered aluminum foil. Brush the top with an egg yolk diluted with some water. Bake at 325° for 45 minutes. Keeps for about one week.

Baniga (Ricotta strudel—recipe from Bulgaria)

THE DOUGH:

>   2 cups flour
>   3 eggs
>   5 tablespoons oil
>   Pinch of salt
>   Some warm water
>   ⅓ pound melted butter

THE FILLING:

>   1 pound ricotta
>   4 eggs
>   ½ cup honey
>   4 tablespoons sugar
>   3 ounces butter
>   Grated peel of half a lemon

Mix the flour, eggs, oil, salt, and water in a blender or by hand. Let rest for ½ hour, then divide the dough in 8 parts and roll each part very thin. Let dry. For the filling: Beat the butter and the eggs together. Add the honey, sugar, salt, grated lemon peel, and ricotta and beat for ½ minute. Line a loaf pan with buttered aluminum foil. Place a layer of dough on the bottom. Brush with the melted butter, spread ¼ of the filling over it, and cover with another layer of dough. Repeat 3 times. Brush the top layer with butter and seal well at the edges. Bake at 350° for 45 minutes. Cut the cake in slices when still warm, serve warm or cold with sour cream.

Bonissima (recipe from Modena)

>   1 recipe Pâte Sucré (sweet pie crust dough)
>   1½ cups honey
>   ½ cup ground walnuts
>   1 teaspoon rum

Place the walnuts, honey and rum in a bowl and mix well. Divide the pie dough in two and use half of the amount to line an 8-inch round pan lined with aluminum foil. Fill with the walnut mixture and cover completely using the leftover dough. Pinch at the edges to seal well. Bake at 350° for 45 minutes or until golden. When cooled, cover with semi-sweet chocolate melted in a double boiler or with a honey glaze.

Cicerchiata *(Carnival recipe from Umbria)*

2 cups honey
4 ounces peeled shredded almonds
2 ounces candied fruits, ground
2 tablespoons olive oil
1 cup flour
2 tablespoons cognac
Grated peel of ½ lemon
4 whole eggs
1 egg yolk

Beat the eggs in a bowl, add the oil, liqueur, and lemon peel. Add enough flour to obtain a soft dough. Blend well and shape into balls the size of a hazelnut. Deep-fry them in hot oil and drain them. Boil the honey in a pan until a drop in a glass of cold water immediately hardens. Remove from heat and place the balls in the honey together with the candied fruits and almonds. Mix well. Grease a ring mold with some oil and pour mixture in it. Remove from mold when cooled.

Cheese Pie

1 recipe Pâte Brisée (pie crust dough), halfway cooked
⅔ pound ricotta cheese or cream cheese
½ pint heavy cream
Grated peel of one lemon
2 eggs
½ cup honey
1 tablespoon lemon juice

Blend all ingredients together. Pour into a 10-inch pie plate lined with the pie crust. Bake at 350° for 20 minutes. If desired, place a layer of fruits in syrup on the bottom. This pie should be served cool with a sauce made with raspberry or blackberry jam, thinned by a few spoons of water or liqueur.

Honey and Cocoa "Panforte"

4 ounces peeled almonds
4 ounces toasted hazelnuts
4 ounces cocoa
½ cup candied ground orange
1½ cups honey
½ cup water
2 teaspoons cinnamon
Grated peel of 1 orange
½ cup flour
4 ounces candied cherries
¾ cup sugar
Confectioner's sugar

Place the honey, sugar, and water in a saucepan. Cook at low heat until a drop of this mixture placed in a glass of cold water forms a rubbery ball. Add all other ingredients and mix well. Pour the mixture into a 9-inch round pan lined with buttered aluminum foil. Bake at 300° for 30 minutes. Cool. Dust with confectioner's sugar.

Apple Tart

1 recipe Pâte Sucré (sweet pie crust dough)
6 golden apples
½ pint heavy cream
Juice of 1 lemon
½ cup acacia honey
1 teaspoon powdered cinnamon
Pinch of nutmeg

Divide the dough in two parts. Line a 10-inch round pan with buttered aluminum foil and spread half the dough in it. Peel and slice the apples and place them in the pan. In a bowl, mix the honey, lemon juice, spices, and heavy cream, and pour over the apples. With the leftover dough, cover the mixture completely and pinch the edges to seal it. Bake at 375° for 1 hour. Remove from pan when cooled.

Cake Grenoble Style

1 recipe Pâte Brisée (pie crust dough)
½ cup acacia honey
1 pint heavy cream
2 eggs
4 tablespoons confectioner's sugar
2 tablespoons kirsch
4 ounces ground walnuts
1 teaspoon powdered cinnamon
1 tablespoon vanilla sugar
Pinch of ginger
1 egg white
12 walnut kernels

Line a 10-inch pan with the pie dough. Beat the eggs, heavy cream, honey, walnuts, cinnamon, ginger, and vanilla sugar. Pour the mixture into the pan. Bake at 350° for 35 minutes. Let cool. In a blender, or by hand, mix the sifted confectioner's sugar, egg white, and the kirsch. Spread the mixture over the cake, decorate with the kernels, and let cool.

Apricot Sticks

1 cup ground dried apricots
½ cup ground walnuts
2 eggs
1¼ cups honey

Beat the eggs with the honey, add the walnuts and the apricots, and blend for another ½ minute. Shape this mixture into small sticks and place over a cookie sheet lined with buttered aluminum foil. Bake at 350° for 10 minutes.

Bran Muffins with Walnuts and Honey

1 cup flour
½ teaspoon baking soda
½ teaspoon salt
1½ cups bran
1 cup honey
1½ cups milk
¼ cup ground walnuts

Sift the flour with the baking soda and the salt. Add the other ingredients and mix until well blended together. Grease some muffin molds, pour the mixture into them, and bake at 400° for 25–30 minutes.

Honey and Oats Cookies

    4 ounces oats
    ½ cup honey
    2 tablespoons sugar
    2 ounces ground almonds
    2 ounces candied fruits
    1 teaspoon powdered cinnamon
    1 teaspoon baking powder
    2 tablespoons water

Blend all ingredients together in a blender or by hand until soft and even. Cover a cookie sheet with buttered aluminum foil. Mold the mixture into walnut-sized balls and place on the sheets. Bake at 350° for 10 minutes. The cookies must have a golden color.

Ricotta and Honey Cakes

    1 container yogurt
    4 tablespoons ricotta cheese
    ½ cup honey
    ¼ cup ground walnuts

Mix the ricotta with the yogurt and place in a strainer overnight to drain. Shape the mixture into flat balls and place them on a cookie sheet lined with buttered aluminum foil. Bake at 325° until dry and hard. Let cool, then brush with the honey and sprinkle with walnuts.

Honey Drops

    ½ cup acacia or eucalyptus honey
    4 eggs, separated
    ½ cup flour

Mix the egg yolks with the honey and fold in the sifted flour rapidly. Beat the egg whites until stiff, and fold lightly into the mixture. Line a cookie sheet with buttered aluminum foil. By spoonfuls, drop the mixture on the sheet. Bake at 325° until golden. When still warm, glaze each drop with a teaspoon of liquid honey.

Honey Madelaines

    2 eggs, separated
    ½ cup honey
    1 tablespoon melted butter
    1 teaspoon orange water or vanilla
        sugar
    ½ cup flour

Mix the egg yolks with the honey. Add the butter and the orange water (or vanilla sugar) , then add the sifted flour. Beat the egg whites until stiff and fold them lightly into the mixture. Pour the mixture in buttered Madelaine molds. Bake at 325° until golden.

Honey Amaretti

    2 egg whites
    ½ cup honey
    4 ounces peeled crushed almonds
    4 ounces peeled crushed hazelnuts

Beat the egg whites until very stiff, add the honey while still beating. Add the almonds and hazelnuts, folding them in lightly with a spatula. Line a cookie sheet with aluminum foil, spoon small amounts of the mixture, and bake at 300° until golden.

Honey Sabbiosi

    2¼ cups flour
    8 ounces butter at room temperature
    ½ cup honey
    2 egg yolks
    Pinch of salt

Mix all ingredients in a blender or by hand until the dough is soft and smooth. Let rest for 1 hour, then roll into a very thin layer over a slightly floured surface. Shape it into lozenges or circles using a dough cutter or a knife. Place these shapes over a cookie sheet lined with aluminum foil. Bake at 350° for 10 minutes. They must have a light golden color.

Cookies Stuffed with Honey

4 ounces mixed crushed candied fruits
¾ cup flour
9 tablespoons butter
3 egg yolks
Some thick honey

Remove the butter from the refrigerator an hour before using it. Blend rapidly, in a blender or by hand, all ingredients except the honey. Roll the dough very thin and cut into small discs. Place on a cookie sheet lined with aluminum foil. Bake at 350° until golden (10–15 minutes). As soon as removed from the oven, spread some honey on one side of half the discs and cover with the other half. The heat of the cookies will melt the honey and the discs will stick together as a sandwich.

Small Almond Tarts

1 recipe Pâte Sucré (sweet pie crust dough)
1 cup cane sugar
8 ounces butter
1 cup honey
8 ounces slivered almonds

Prepare the pie dough and spread it. Cut into small circles and line small molds previously buttered. Place the sugar, honey, and butter in a pan and bring to a boil. Add the almonds. Mix well and remove from heat. When cooled, pour a spoonful of this mixture in each mold. Bake at 375° until golden (about 20 minutes). Remove from molds when cooled.

Pan Melati (recipe from Umbria)

2 cups bread crumbs
8 ounces crushed walnuts
2 teaspoons cinnamon
2 cups honey
1 orange peel

Cut the orange peel into cubes and place with the honey in a saucepan. When the honey starts to melt and begins to boil, add the bread crumbs, cinnamon, and walnuts. Mix well with a wooden spoon. Cook for 5 minutes, then pour the mixture over a marble or oiled surface and let cool. Cut in 2-inch pieces and mold into small balls.

Honey Sticks

1¼ cups honey
1 cup confectioner's sugar
8 ounces peeled almonds, cut in half
1½ cups flour
1 tablespoon crushed candied citron
Pinch powdered nutmeg
Pinch powdered cloves
¼ cup lemon juice

Place the honey and sugar in a saucepan. Bring to a boil and add the almonds and mix well. Spread the mixture ½ inch thick over aluminum foil. When cooled, wrap in aluminum foil for 12 hours. Place on a cookie sheet lined with buttered aluminum foil. Bake at 350° for 20 minutes. Remove and cut into 1″ x 2″ sticks. Glaze as you prefer.

Spice Cookies

½ cup crushed hazelnuts
2½ cups flour
7 tablespoons butter
½ cup cane sugar
A few tablespoons milk
¾ cup honey
2 eggs
1 tablespoon baking soda
3 teaspoons cinnamon
4 tablespoons allspice

Blend all ingredients in a blender until you have a smooth dough. Roll to a 2-inch thickness on a lightly floured surface. Cut into any shapes of your choice and place on a cookie sheet lined with aluminum foil. Bake at 350° for 10–15 minutes.

Hansel and Gretel Gingerbread House

2 pounds flour
½ pound butter
1 cup honey
½ pound cane sugar
2 teaspoons allspice
1 egg
1 teaspoon baking soda
½ tablespoon salt
2 teaspoons cinnamon
3 tablespoons milk

Blend all ingredients in a blender until the mixture is soft and smooth. Spread the mixture over a slightly floured surface and cut out for the house: 2 fronts, 2 roofs, and 2 sides. Place the different pieces on a cookie sheet lined with aluminum foil. Bake at 350° for about 10 minutes. When cooled, assemble with a thick glaze forming a house you can decorate with walnuts, candies or chopped pistachios.

GLAZE:
Mix in a blender ⅓ pound confectioner's sugar and an egg white. When the mixture is dense and shiny, remove. Use before it hardens.

Simple Mostaccioli (recipe from Calabria)

2¼ cups flour
1¼ cups honey
½ glass anise liqueur (Sambuca or other)

Blend the flour with the honey and liqueur (in a blender or by hand) . Roll to ¼-inch thickness over a slightly floured surface. Cut in different shapes and place them on a cookie sheet lined with buttered aluminum foil. Bake at 325° until golden. Use after a few days as they will be crispier.

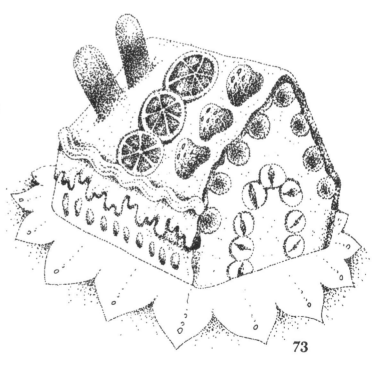

73

Pepatelli (recipe from Abruzzo)

1¼ cups honey
8 ounces crushed peeled almonds
Grated peel of 1 orange
2 teaspoons pepper
Some whole wheat flour

Place the honey in a pan, bring to boil mixing constantly. Add the almonds, orange peel, pepper, and enough flour to obtain a thick mixture. Mix well. Pour the mixture to a 2-inch thickness on a cookie sheet lined with aluminum foil. Let cool, cut into rectangles 2½ inches long. Place them on another cookie sheet lined with buttered aluminum foil. Bake at 325° until golden. Serve with a sweet wine. These keep for a long time.

Taralli (recipe from Calabria)

1¼ cups flour
4 tablespoons honey
1 tablespoon yeast
2 eggs
3 tablespoons olive oil

Prepare a bread dough using water, yeast, and the flour. Let rise and add the eggs, oil, and honey. Mix well. Shape into doughnut shapes. Place on a cookie sheet lined with buttered aluminum foil. Let rise for 3–4 hours. Bake at 350° until golden.

Straca Dent (recipe from Emilia-Romagna)

1 1/5 pound peeled almonds
2 cups honey
1 cup flour
3 egg whites

Cut the almonds in half lengthwise, mix with the honey, and add the flour. Beat the egg whites until very stiff, then fold lightly into the mixture. With a spoon, drop small amounts of the mixture on a cookie sheet lined with buttered aluminum foil. Bake at 325° until golden. Remove from sheet when cooled.

Panafracchi (recipe from Venezia Giulia)

4 cups flour
2½ cups honey
4 ounces crushed almonds
1 tablespoon powdered coriander
Grated peel of 1 lemon
½ cup sugar
4 ounces crushed pinoli (pine) nuts
¾ cup oil
Pinch of saffron
Pinch of salt
Pinch of nutmeg
Pinch of cinnamon
½ cup Marsala wine (or sweet white wine)

Melt the sugar, honey, and oil in a pan. Add the almonds and pine nuts. Pour this mixture into a blender; add all other ingredients and mix. Work well until the dough is smooth and soft. Spread out and shape into circles hollow at the center. Place on a cookie sheet lined with greased aluminum foil. Let rest for 12 hours. Bake at 350° for 30 minutes. When cooled, place in a tin box and use after one week.

Zeppole (recipe from Campania)

4 cups flour
1 cup honey
4 ounces anise seeds
Grated peel of 1 lemon
Oil
Salt

Boil 4 pints of water in a pan together with the lemon peel and a tablespoon of salt. Add the flour through a sifter and cook for 15 minutes, mixing constantly. The mixture must be thick and smooth. Pour it on an oiled surface and knead into a long cylinder. Cut into thin slices using an oiled knife. Deep-fry a few at a time. Drain them over paper, then dip them in honey and sprinkle the anise seeds over them. Zeppole are usually made for Christmas.

Turdilli *(recipe from Calabria)*

> **2 cups oil**
> **1 cup white wine**
> **1½ cups flour**
> **¾ cup honey**
> **1 teaspoon cinnamon**
> **Grated peel of 1 orange**

Mix in a blender the flour, oil, wine, cinnamon, and orange peel. When thoroughly mixed, remove, divide in four parts and shape into thick cylinders. Cut into 2-inch sticks and grate. Fry a few at a time over low heat. When golden, remove and drain. Soak into a syrup obtained by boiling the honey and ¼ cup water. Drain after 5 minutes.

Cavallucci

> **½ cup honey**
> **2 tablespoons cane sugar**
> **1 tablespoon crushed candied citron**
> **¾ cup flour**
> **1 tablespoon baking powder**
> **2 tablespoons anise seeds**
> **2 tablespoons kirsch or sambuca liqueur**

Melt the honey with the sugar, then add the flour and baking powder sifted together. Mix in a blender or by hand, using a wooden spoon. Add the citron, anise seeds, and the liqueur. Spread the dough and cut into squares. Place on a cookie sheet lined with aluminum foil. Bake at 375° for 15 minutes. Will keep indefinitely in an airtight box.

Christmas Rings *(recipe from Belgium)*

> **1½ cups sifted flour**
> **½ teaspoon sifted baking soda**
> **¼ pound soft butter**
> **1½ cups lukewarm water**
> **4 egg yolks**
> **¼ pound cocoa**
> **¼ pound sugar**
> **1 tablespoon crushed almonds**
> **Grated peel of 1 orange**
> **1 teaspoon cinnamon**

Place all ingredients in a blender and mix until the mixture is smooth. Roll the dough over a slightly floured surface and cut into small circles. Place on a cookie sheet lined with aluminum foil and brush them with a beaten egg white. Bake at 350° for 10–15 minutes.

Baklava (*Turkish cookies*)

THE DOUGH:
- 1½ cups sifted flour
- 4 eggs
- 1 teaspoon salt
- Cold water
- Oil

THE FILLING:
- 1 cup peeled and crushed almonds
- 4 ounces crushed pistachios
- 4 ounces crushed pinoli (pine nuts)
- 1½ cups honey
- 4 ounces crushed hazelnuts
- 1 cup confectioner's sugar
- 10 ounces butter

Place the flour, eggs, salt, water, and oil in a blender and blend until the mixture is soft. Shape into small balls, flatten with a rolling pin over a floured board until round and very thin. Mix the almonds, pistachios, pine nuts, hazelnuts, and sugar. Drop a spoonful of this mixture at the center of each cookie, previously brushed with butter. Fold the disc in two and seal at the edges. Deep-fry in boiling oil, drain, and dip them in boiling honey. Drain and let cool.

Bedouin's Delight (*recipe from Morocco*)

- 1 cup flour
- 1½ teaspoons baking powder
- 3 tablespoons sugar
- 1 teaspoon salt
- ¼ pound butter
- 2 cups honey
- 8 ounces ground pitted dates
- 8 ounces almonds
- 3 eggs
- 1 tablespoon peanut oil

Sift the flour with the baking powder and salt, add the dates and almonds. Beat the eggs until foamy, then add the sugar, oil, and honey. Pour all ingredients in the blender and mix well. Pour in a rectangular cake pan lined with greased aluminum foil. Bake at 350° until golden. Cut into 6 parts when still warm and sprinkle each part with confectioner's sugar.

Honey Lebkuchen

1 ounce potassium carbonate (you
    can find it in a drug store)
3 tablespoons rum or Marsala wine
1 teaspoon powdered cinnamon
½ teaspoon powdered cloves
1 pound sugar
1 cup honey
4 cups flour
4 ounces crushed candied fruits
4 eggs
12 ounces crushed almonds

Melt the potassium carbonate in the wine.
Sift flour and spices and add the candied
fruits. Place all ingredients in a blender
and mix well. Roll to a ¼-inch thickness
over a floured surface. Cut into 2″ x 3″
rectangles. Place on a cookie sheet lined
with buttered aluminum foil. Keep in a
cool place for 12 hours. Bake at 325° for
25 minutes.

Lekerles (Kirsch cookies—recipe from Switzerland)

2 cups flour
1½ cups liquid honey
1 cup sugar
4 ounces crushed almonds
1 egg
4 ounces candied orange, lemon, and
    citron peels
1 tablespoon powdered cinnamon
1 teaspoon powdered cloves
¼ cup kirsch
1 tablespoon baking powder

Mix all ingredients in a blender, shape
the dough into a ball, wrap it in a damp
cloth, and keep for 12 hours in a cool place.
Divide the dough in 4 parts, roll it out,
and shape into a very thin rectangle. Place
over a cookie sheet lined with aluminum
foil. Bake at 350° for 10 minutes. When
still warm, cut into 2″ x 3″ rectangles.
Prepare a glaze with confectioner's sugar
and some water; use it to brush the cookies.

Pistachios and Honey Kipfel

THE DOUGH

  1 tablespoon yeast
  ¼ cup cold water
  ½ pound butter
  ½ cup sugar
  2 cups flour
  3 eggs
  1 teaspoon salt
  Grated peel of ½ lemon
  ¾ cup lukewarm milk

THE FILLING:

  ¾ cup crushed pistachios
  ½ cup honey
  ¼ cup cane sugar

Melt the yeast in lukewarm water. Mix the butter with the sugar (in a blender or by hand using a wooden spoon). Add the eggs one at a time, then the salt, lemon peel, yeast, lukewarm milk, and flour. Mix well. Cover the dough with a cloth, place in a warm place, and let rise until it is double in bulk. Mix the sugar and pistachios and add enough honey to obtain a smooth mixture. Roll the dough ¼″ thick over a floured surface. Cut into 3½″ squares. Place a spoonful of filling at the center and fold the squares in half, sealing well at the edges. Place on a cookie sheet lined with buttered aluminum foil. Let rise. Bake at 350° until golden.

Yak Kwa (Honey Flowers—recipe from Korea)

2 tablespoons honey
2 tablespoons sherry
1 teaspoon almond extract
2 tablespoons water
¾ pound flour
2 tablespoons oil
1 cup water
1½ cups honey

Mix in a pan 2 tablespoons honey, sherry, almond extract, 2 tablespoons water, cook at low heat for 5 minutes, mixing constantly. Let cool, then add the sifted flour and the oil. Mix well. Roll the dough on a floured surface until very thin. Cut into flower shapes or small discs. Mix the water and the honey in a pan and cook at very low heat for 5 minutes, stirring often. Let this syrup cool. Deep-fry the flowers or discs a few at a time in hot oil until they float. Drain and let dry on paper, then drop them in the honey syrup. Soak for at least 24 hours; they will become deliciously crisp.

Chocolate Pernik (recipe from Czechoslovakia)

1 pound whole wheat flour
¼ pound sugar
3 tablespoons cocoa
1 teaspoon baking soda
¼ teaspoon mace
½ teaspoon powdered cloves
3 tablespoons milk
¼ teaspoon allspice
1 teaspoon cinnamon
1 egg
¾ cup lukewarm honey
Pinch of salt
7 tablespoons butter
4 ounces semi-sweet chocolate

Sift the flour, baking soda, and spices. Place all ingredients in a blender and mix well. Keep the dough overnight covered with a cloth. Spread on a cookie sheet lined with buttered aluminum foil; the dough must be ½-inch thick. Bake at 325° for 10 minutes. Melt the semi-sweet chocolate and use as a glaze. Cut into squares. These cookies will keep for a few months if kept in a tin box.

Walnut and Honey Cookies

1 cup honey
2 tablespoons vegetable oil
¾ teaspoon baking soda
½ teaspoon salt
1 tablespoon warm water
1¾ cups flour
4 ounces crushed walnuts

Blend rapidly all ingredients in a blender. Shape into a cylinder, wrap in aluminum foil, and place in the freezer for 1 hour. When hard, cut into thin slices with a sharp knife. Place the slices 1 inch apart on a buttered cookie sheet. Bake at 350° for 10 minutes.

Tasty Mostaccioli (recipe from Calabria)

2 cups honey
½ cup toasted crushed almonds
1 cup sugar
2 cups flour
1 teaspoon cinnamon
4 eggs
Grated peel of 2 oranges
1 teaspoon powdered cloves

Heat the honey in a saucepan. Place all ingredients in a blender and pour the honey over it. Mix well. Roll into finger-thick cylinders 6 inches long, and shape as a doughnut. Place on a cookie sheet lined with buttered aluminum foil and let sit overnight. Bake at 350° until golden.

Zeppole (recipe from Abruzzi)

1 cup flour
1 teaspoon semolina
4 egg yolks
¾ cup honey
1 bay leaf
Pinch of salt
2 tablespoons butter or shortening
2 cups water

Boil the water in a pan with the honey, butter, bay leaf, and salt. Remove from heat, then add the flour and semolina. Mix rapidly with a wooden spoon, place again on flame. Cook for 7–8 minutes, stirring constantly. Remove the bay leaf, let cool, then add the egg yolks and mix well. Shape into rings and fry, pricking them now and then with a fork. When golden and crisp, remove, strain, and sprinkle with confectioner's sugar.

PUDDINGS

How To Coat a Mold with Honey

Bring the honey to a boil. It will become a light foam. Keep boiling while watching that it does not boil over (it behaves a bit like milk) until dark and thick. Remove from heat and let cool. Pour in the mold and proceed as with caramel; the only difference is that it will take more time as honey hardens more slowly. Make sure that all sides are evenly coated.

Cooked Honey Cream

> 4 cups milk
> 6 eggs
> ½ cup honey
> ¼ teaspoon salt
> Nutmeg

Melt the honey and milk in a pan. Separately, beat the eggs with an electric beater, add the milk and honey, and keep beating. Add the salt. Pour the mixture in individual ceramic molds or in a large ring mold, coated with honey. Sprinkle some nutmeg on the surface. Bake at $325°$ over a pan with water for one hour. Serve warm or cold.

Honey Mousse

> 5 eggs, separated
> 1¾ cup honey
> 1 tablespoon vanilla sugar

Place the egg yolks, honey, and sugar in a saucepan and beat with an electric mixer for a few seconds. Bring the mixture to a boil while mixing. Lower the flame and let cook, while still beating, for about 5 minutes (the mixture must double in bulk). Pour in a bowl and let cool. Beat the egg whites until stiff and fold lightly into the mixture. Pour the mousse in a glass bowl or in individual bowls and refrigerate for at least 2 hours before serving.

Honey Pudding

1 cup sifted flour
1½ teaspoons sifted baking powder
8 eggs
¾ cup sugar
½ cup honey

Beat the eggs with an electric beater, then add the honey and sugar. Beat until stiff. Add the flour and baking powder and mix with a wooden spoon. When perfectly blended, pour the mixture in a buttered ring mold. Bake at 350° for 45 minutes. Remove from mold when cooled. Serve with fresh fruits or whipped cream or, even better, with a honey cream.

Poor Rider's Cake (French Toast)

2 eggs
2 tablespoons honey
¼ teaspoon powdered cinnamon
¾ cup milk
4–6 slices dry white bread
1 teaspoon butter

Beat the eggs, add the cinnamon, milk, and honey. Trim the crust from the bread, then cut the slices in half and soak in the mixture. Drain quickly, butter on both sides, and sautée in a skillet. Serve warm with a honey cream.

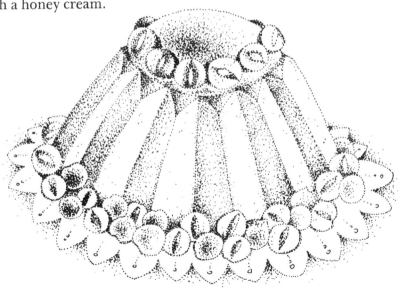

Potato and Honey Cake

1 cup flour
½ pound potatoes, boiled with the
   skins, then mashed
½ cup honey
2 tablespoons melted butter
½ tablespoon baking powder
¼ teaspoon cinnamon

Place all ingredients in a blender and mix well (can also be done by hand). Roll the dough on a lightly floured surface to about a 3-inch thickness. Place on a rectangular pan lined with aluminum foil. Bake at 400° until golden (about 30 minutes). When ready, cut into squares.

Banana Pudding

4 bananas
2 cups milk
½ cup honey
2 tablespoons corn starch
2 eggs
Pinch of nutmeg

Peel and slice the bananas. Place in a buttered oven dish. Bring the milk and honey to a boil in a pan, add the corn starch, melted in a bit of cold milk. Beat the eggs and add to the milk, mixing constantly. Pour the mixture over the banana slices. Bake at 325° for 20 minutes until golden. Serve cold.

Prune Pudding

⅔ pound pitted prunes
1 tablespoon lemon juice
¼ tablespoon powdered cloves
4 egg whites
Pinch of salt
¼ cup honey

Beat the prunes with the lemon juice and cloves. Beat the egg whites, and add the salt and honey while still beating. Fold the egg whites lightly into the prune mixture. Butter a 1½-quart ring mold, sprinkle with confectioner's sugar, and pour the mixture in it. Bake at 350° over a pan of water for 45 minutes. Serve hot or cold.

Grand Marnier Honey Mousse

2 pounds apples
½ acacia or orange honey
6 egg whites
¼ cup Grand Marnier
Honey for glaze

Peel and slice the apples. Bake at 400° until soft. When ready, mash them, add the honey, and let this mixture dry in a pan over high flame for a few minutes. Let cool. Beat the egg whites until very stiff, add to the apple mixture, and finally add the Grand Marnier. Pour the mixture in a ring mold glazed with honey. Place in the oven over a pan of water and bake at 350° for about 30 minutes. Serve this mousse warm or cold with a honey cream or orange marmalade diluted with some warm water.

Bread and Honey Pudding

6 slices rye bread
¼ pound raisins
3 cups warm milk
¼ teaspoon nutmeg
½ pound honey
¼ teaspoon allspice
1 teaspoon powdered cinnamon
2 eggs, beaten

Cut each slice of bread in four parts. Place them in a buttered oven dish. Sprinkle with raisins soaked in warm water for 15 minutes. Mix the milk, spices, and honey separately and gradually mix with the beaten eggs. Pour the mixture over the bread. Bake at 320° for 35–40 minutes or until golden and crisp.

Pumpkin Cake

1¾ pounds pumpkin
1 cup water
1 cup milk
1 tablespoon butter
2 eggs
4 tablespoons flour
1 cup warm water
½ cup sunflower honey
1 tablespoon melted honey
Honey to glaze the mold

Cook the pumpkin with the water and honey in a covered pan. When tender, grind in a food mill. Melt the butter with the honey, add the flour and the warm water. Add the mashed pumpkin and cook, mixing constantly, until the mixture is thick. Let cool. Add the egg yolks and remaining ingredients, and finally fold in the egg whites, beaten stiff. Pour the mixture in a ring mold glazed with honey. Bake at 325° for 20 minutes.

Bread and Honey Meringue Pie

1 loaf stale bread (without the crust)
½ cup milk
½ cup boiling water
3 eggs, separated
½ cup honey
1 tablespoon butter (at room temperature)
2 tablespoons sugar

Soak the bread in the milk and water. Beat the egg yolks and add the honey and butter. Mix well and add to the bread. Pour the mixture in a buttered oven dish. Bake at 350° for 30–40 minutes. Beat the egg whites until very stiff, spread on the surface of the pudding, sprinkle with the sugar, and bake at 400° for 10 minutes.

Glazed Rice Pudding

4 ounces rice
2 cups milk
½ cup honey
½ cup raisins
1 teaspoon butter
2 egg yolks

Soak the raisins in some water. Cook the rice in boiling water for 3 minutes and drain. Place it in an oven dish with the milk, cover with aluminum foil, and bake at 400° until the milk has been completely absorbed. Be careful, though, not to burn it. Beat the egg yolks, add the honey and butter, then add the rice and mix well. Add the drained and dried raisins, and pour the mixture in a ring mold with a capacity of about 2 pints. The mold must be glazed with honey. Bake over a pan of water at 350° for 20 minutes. This can be served warm with cooked fruits or cold with pineapple cubes or whipped cream.

Semolina and Marsala Pudding

½ cup semolina
½ cup liquid honey
2 ounces candied citron, cut into cubes
1 ounce raisins, soaked in water for 15 minutes
1 small glass Marsala wine
2½ ounces pistachios, crushed
1 quart milk
2 eggs, separated
2 egg yolks
Grated peel of 1 lemon

Bring the milk to a boil in a saucepan, add the semolina, sifting it, and let cook for 10 minutes, while mixing constantly with a wooden spoon. When the mixture has cooled, add the beaten egg yolks, wine, honey, citron, pistachios, raisins, lemon peel, and finally the egg whites, beaten stiff. Mix well and pour in a tube pan with a capacity of 2 pints, buttered and sprinkled with semolina. Bake at 350° for 40 minutes. Remove from pan placing it on a dish, and serve warm with a honey cream.

Honey Roulade

THE DOUGH:

>4 eggs, separated
>1 tablespoon flour
>1 tablespoon acacia honey

THE FILLING:

>⅓ pound Mascarpone cheese (or
>   cream cheese)
>½ pint heavy cream
>4 ounces crushed walnuts or pistachios
>8 kernels of whole walnuts
>½ cup liquid acacia honey

Place the egg yolks in a bowl and beat with a wooden spoon. When foamy, add the honey and beat some more, add the flour, and finally the egg whites, beaten until very stiff. Pour the mixture in a rectangular oven dish, measuring 12″ x 14″ lined with buttered aluminum foil. Bake at 350° for 15–20 minutes. When ready, turn the oven dish upside down, placing a sheet of aluminum foil under it, to remove the roulade. When cool, unroll and spread with the filling prepared by mixing the cheese, nuts, honey, and cream. Roll again and place in the refrigerator wrapped in aluminum foil for a few hours. Shortly before serving, remove the paper, place the roulade on a serving dish, and decorate with whipped cream and walnut kernels.

Apples and Honey Charlotte

>1 tablespoon butter
>½ cup bread crumbs
>1 1/5 pounds apples
>Grated peel and juice of ½ lemon
>½ cup honey
>1 tablespoon water
>1 teaspoon cinnamon
>¼ teaspoon powdered cloves

Butter the bottom and sides of an eight-inch-round pan. Sprinkle a thick layer of bread crumbs, and press. Peel the apples, cut in slices and place in the pan in layers, alternating layers of apple and bread crumbs. The last layer must be of bread crumbs. In a sauce pan place the lemon peel and juice, honey and water, at low heat mixing constantly until well blended. Pour this syrup over the top layer of bread crumbs and bake at 325° for one hour. Serve with cream or honey cream.

Apple Mousse with Cream

1⅔ pounds apples
1 teaspoon butter
1 vanilla bean
3 tablespoons water
½ cup honey
1 pint heavy cream
1 ounce confectioner's sugar

Peel and cube the apples, place in a pan with the butter, vanilla and water. Cover and cook at very low heat until the apples are completely soft, almost mashed. Mix well, then add the honey, mix and keep cooking until the honey has melted. Let cool, then remove the vanilla bean. Whip the cream, adding two tablespoons confectioner's sugar. Pour the apple mixture in a glass bowl, then add the whipped cream. Refrigerate for at least three hours and serve decorated with crushed walnuts.

Winnie the Pooh's Soufflé

6 eggs, separated
¼ teaspoon salt
2 tablespoons sugar
1 cup chestnut honey
½ tablespoon allspice
Grated peel of 1 lemon
2 tablespoons flour
2 tablespoons melted butter

Beat the egg yolks until foamy, add the honey, lemon peel, the sifted flour and the butter. Continue to beat. Beat the egg whites with the salt until stiff, add the sugar and beat some more. Fold lightly into the egg yolks. Pour in a one and a half quart soufflé dish. Bake at 350° for thirty minutes, until golden. Serve immediately with whipped cream and grated chocolate.

Raspberries Roulade

THE DOUGH:
- 4 eggs
- 1 cup honey
- 1 tablespoon flour
- 2 teaspoons baking powder
- ¼ teaspoon baking soda

THE FILLING:
- 1 cup raspberries
- ½ cup sugar
- 4 tablespoons corn starch

Beat the eggs, add the honey then the flour, baking powder and baking soda sifted together. Pour the mixture in a rectangular oven dish, lined with buttered aluminum foil, bake at 320° for twenty-five minutes. Remove, turn dish upside down, place the roulade over aluminum foil sprinkled with confectioner's sugar. Delicately remove from the aluminum foil and roll the roulade on itself. Let cool. Beat the raspberries, add the sugar, and bring to a boil in a pan. Melt the corn starch in some water, add to the raspberries, let cook at very low heat for a few minutes. Let cool. Unroll the roulade, spread the raspberries mixture over it, roll again. Serve, if you wish, with whipped cream.

Honey Couscous

- 2¼ pounds couscous
- ½ cup liquid honey
- ⅓ pound pitted crushed dates
- ¼ pound raisins, soaked in warm water for 30 minutes
- ¼ pound crushed almonds
- 1 tablespoon butter
- 1 pinch saffron
- 1 tablespoon vanilla sugar

Heat the couscous in a double boiler, add the butter and let melt. Mix separately all other ingredients, mixing lightly. Pour in a bowl and serve.

Pannuka Kku (*Finnish Crêpes*)

- 2 ounces butter
- 2 eggs
- 2 tablespoons honey
- ¼ teaspoon salt
- 1¾ cups milk
- ½ cup flour

Place in an eight-inch-round pan one ounce butter, melt in the oven at 400°
In the meantime beat the eggs, honey, salt, milk, butter and flour. Pour the mixture in the pan and bake at 400° for about twenty minutes. It must be golden and puffy. Cut and serve sprinkled with confectioner's sugar or with sour cream, strawberries and cane sugar.

Swedish Rice Crêpes

½ cup rice
1 pint milk
1 pinch salt
1½ tablespoons honey
3 eggs
Pinch of nutmeg

Place the rice, milk, salt and honey in a double boiler. Cook while mixing occasionally, until the rice has absorbed the milk and has become creamy (about 2 hours). Let cool, beat the eggs, then add the rice and nutmeg. Heat a skillet, oiled with some butter, pour a spoonful of the mixture and fry on both sides over low heat. Serve the crêpes with strawberry jam or a honey cream.

Rice with Dried Fruit

¾ cup rice
¾ cup water
¾ cup milk
⅓ pound dried fruit (prunes, apricots, or peaches)
2 tablespoons honey
Pinch of salt
1 vanilla bean
2 ounces butter

Soak the dried fruit in water for twelve hours. Place in a pan the rice, water, milk, vanilla, and a pinch of salt. Cover and cook over very low heat about twenty minutes or until the rice is tender and has absorbed all liquids. Add the honey, cook for five more minutes over high flame, then remove the vanilla bean. Cook the fruit with the water in which it soaked and two table-spoons of honey for five minutes over high flame. Reserve the syrup, mash the fruit. Place in a buttered oven dish layers of rice and mashed fruit, the last layer must be of rice. Place some butter on the top, pour on the syrup, and bake at 350° for ten minutes.

CANDIES

Coconut Candies

    1 tablespoon butter
    1 cup honey
    Pinch of salt
    1 cup grated coconut
    1 tablespoon sugar
    1 teaspoon vanilla

Place the honey and salt in a pan, bring to boil mixing occasionally, until the mixture is thick. Remove pan from flame and add almost all of the coconut and the vanilla and sugar, this mixture must be very stiff. Butter a rectangular oven dish and sprinkle well with coconut. Pour the mixture in the pan spreading it with a knife. Cover with the leftover coconut and cut into small squares before it hardens.

Apple and Honey Candies

    2 cups acacia honey
    ½ cup applesauce
    1 ounce butter
    ½ pound crushed walnuts

Place the honey and applesauce in a pan, bring to boil over high flame until a drop of the mixture dropped in a glass of cold water forms a small hard ball. Mix constantly to avoid burning. Add the butter and walnuts, and pour in a rectangular oven dish lined with buttered aluminum foil. Cut into small squares while still warm.

Walnut and Date Candies

    ¼ pound butter
    1½ cups honey
    ⅓ pound crushed walnuts
    ¼ pound dates

Place the butter, honey and walnuts in a pan. Cook over low heat mixing constantly, until a drop of the mixture dropped in a glass of cold water forms a small hard ball. Add the dates, and pour the mixture in a rectangular oven dish, lined with aluminum foil and buttered. Cut into squares while still warm. Keep these candies wrapped in aluminum foil.

Homestyle Candies

½ pound chocolate
½ pound sugar
1 cup honey
1 pint heavy cream

Cook all ingredients in a pan for about fifteen minutes, while mixing constantly with a wooden spoon. The mixture will be ready when a drop placed in a glass of cold water turns into a soft ball. Pour the mixture in a square eight-inch oven dish, lined with buttered aluminum foil. When cooled cut into small squares.

Granola

1 pound oats
¼ pound peeled and crushed
    sunflower seeds
4 ounces grated coconut
4 ounces slivered almonds
1 tablespoon powdered cinnamon
1 cup honey
4 tablespoons oil
¼ pound raisins

Mix together the oats, sunflower seeds, coconut, almonds and cinnamon. Mix separately the honey, and oil, add to the first mixture and mix well. Pour the mixture in a rectangular oven dish, lined with aluminum foil and greased lightly with very little oil. Bake at 320° for forty minutes mixing often. Remove, let cool and add the raisins. Very good for breakfast or tea with cold milk or yogurt.

Coffee Candies

½ pound sugar
1 pint heavy cream
½ cup honey
1 tablespoon milk
3 tablespoons of very strong coffee

Place all ingredients in a pan except for the coffee. Cook over low heat for fifteen minutes, then add the coffee. Mix well then pour in a rectangular oven dish, lined with buttered aluminum foil. When it starts to harden cut in small squares.

Simple Honey Nougat

¼ pound almonds
½ pound hazelnuts
¼ pound pistachios
½ cup honey

Place the almonds, hazelnuts and pistachios in the oven and toast lightly. Boil the honey in a pan for ten minutes, add the nuts and cook while mixing all the time. It is ready when a drop of the mixture dropped in a glass of cold water turns into a soft ball. Pour the mixture in a rectangular oven dish, lined with aluminum foil, greased with some oil, spread well using a spatula or a lemon. Let cool and cut with a knife or break in irregular pieces.

Chocolate Nougat

1⅔ pounds peeled hazelnuts
1 pound sugar
1 cup honey
⅓ pound bitter chocolate in pieces
1 cup water
3 egg whites

Melt in a pan two ounces sugar with two ounces water, then add the chocolate and let melt while mixing constantly. Boil the honey separately, until a drop of it dropped in a glass of cold water hardens immediately. Beat the egg whites until very stiff. Cook the rest of the sugar separately with a cup of water, add the honey and mix well. Add the egg whites, then the chocolate and the hazelnuts. Pour the mixture in a rectangular pan lined with wafers or aluminum foil greased with some oil. Spread the mixture one inch thick. When cooled cut in rectangles and wrap them in aluminum foil. It will keep for a long time in a closed container.

Dry Figs Nougat

4 cups honey
1⅓ pounds crushed walnuts
1⅓ pounds dry figs, chopped
1 pound sugar
Grated peel of 1 lemon
2 tablespoons cinnamon
4 egg whites

Cook the honey in a double boiler until it becomes white. Beat the egg whites until very stiff and add to the honey. Continue cooking while mixing all the time. It is ready when a drop of the mixture placed in a glass of water hardens immediately. Add the walnuts, figs, sugar, cinnamon and the lemon peel. Keep cooking and mixing until the mixture thickens. Pour in a rectangular pan, lined with oiled aluminum foil. Roll half inch thick. Cool and cut in rectangles, wrap them in aluminum foil. It will keep for a long time in a closed container.

Tunonis (recipe from Sardinia)

1 cup honey
4 ounces peeled toasted almonds
2 egg whites
Grated peel of ½ lemon

Beat the egg whites until very stiff. Place the honey in a pan, add the egg whites and mix well. Cook over low heat for two hours mixing occasionally. The mixture must become very thick. Add the almonds and lemon peel and mix some more. Pour the mixture in a rectangular pan, lined with oiled aluminum foil, spread and let cool. Cut in small pieces, wrap in aluminum foil, and keep in a closed container.

Christmas Nougat (recipe from Sicily)

    2 cups flour
    1 1/5 pounds peeled crushed almonds
    1/5 pound pinoli (pine) nuts
    2 cups honey
    ½ cup oil
    Peel of 1 lemon
    ½ cup 100-proof rum
    2 teaspoons powdered nutmeg
    Pinch of salt
    Peel of 1 orange
    Peel of 1 tangerine

Bring the oil to a boil with half the peel of the orange, tangerine and lemon, let cool. Place the flour and rum in a mixer and blend for some time. Then add the oil, the remaining peels (grated), salt, nutmeg and mix some more. If the mixture seems to be too thick, add a few drops of lukewarm water, it must become soft and smooth. Let stand for one half hour, then shape into small balls the size of an almond. Fry in boiling oil and drain well. Boil the honey in a pan until it forms a "string." Add the almonds and the fried balls. Mix with a wooden spoon until all the honey has been absorbed and the mixture detaches from the sides of the pan. Pour the mixture in a rectangular pan, lined with oiled aluminum foil. Spread well using a spatula, then sprinkle with pinoli and cinnamon. Cut in small squares before it hardens.

Nuorese Orange (recipe from Sardinia)

    1 1/5 pounds orange peel (without
        the white part)
    1½ cups honey
    4 ounces peeled, toasted and shredded
        almonds
    ½ cup sugar

Cut the orange peel into thin strips. Soak in cold water for two days changing the water twice a day. Drain the peel, dry and weigh. Place in a pan with the equivalent weight of honey, then cook for one half hour over medium heat, mixing all the time. Add the almonds and sugar, cook for five more minutes. Pour the mixture in a pan, lined with oiled aluminum foil, spread and cut in pieces when cooled. It will keep for a few days.

Dates Halva (recipe from India)

1 pound pitted dates
½ pound peeled crushed almonds
6 pods cardamon
4 tablespoons melted butter
2 tablespoons honey

Grind the dates, then soak in one half cup of water for one half hour. Grind again with the water. Open the cardamon pods, remove the black seeds and crush them. Heat two tablespoons of butter in a medium size pan, add the almonds, sauté until golden and reserve. Place in the pan the leftover butter. When warm add the honey, and when it starts to boil add the ground dates. Cook for ten minutes then add the almonds and cardamon, mix well. Pour the mixture in a rectangular pan, greased with butter, spread well with a spatula and cut into squares when cooled.

Honey Nougat (recipe from Cremona)

1 1/5 pounds peeled toasted almonds
¾ cup honey
1 cup sugar
½ pound peeled toasted hazelnuts
4 ounces crushed candied orange and citron
3 egg whites
Grated peel of 2 lemons

Place the honey in a large double boiler, cook for about one and a half hours, stirring frequently. Remove when a drop placed in a glass of cold water hardens immediately. Shortly before the honey is ready place the sugar and one half cup water in a pan and cook, repeat the drop test as above, taking care not to burn. Beat the egg whites until very stiff, add to the honey, while mixing continuously, then add the sugar. When the mixture thickens, add the almonds, hazelnuts, candied fruits, and lemon peel. Mix well. Line a rectangular pan with aluminum foil, greased with very little oil. Pour the mixture into it, spread evenly, cover with more aluminum foil, place a tray with a weight over it and let cool. When ready cut into pieces, wrap them in aluminum foil and keep in a closed container.

Badam Barfi (Almond cookies—recipe from India)

6 cardamon pods
½ pound peeled crushed almonds
2 tablespoons crushed pistachios
¾ cup milk
8 tablespoons honey
3 tablespoons melted butter

Remove the black seeds from the cardamon pods and crush them. Beat the almonds with the milk, pour in a small pan and cook over medium heat for ten minutes, mixing continuously with a wooden spoon. Add the honey, pistachios and butter, continue to cook over low heat, mixing for fifteen to twenty minutes. When the mixture is thick and coarse add the cardamon, mix and pour in a pan lined with buttered aluminum foil. Spread well using a buttered spatula. When cool, cut into small squares. These candies will keep for many weeks if refrigerated and in a closed container.

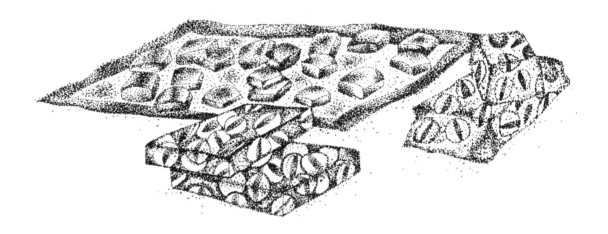

ICE CREAM

Honey Ice Cream

>   4 eggs
>   ½ cup honey
>   1 vanilla bean
>   2 pints heavy cream

Beat the eggs until foamy, add the honey and one pint cream. Cook in a double boiler with the vanilla bean. When the mixture begins to thicken, remove from flame, let cool, remove the vanilla bean and add the rest of the cream, whipped. Pour the mixture in ice trays or in individual bowls and freeze until thick.

Grape Ice Cream

>   ¾ cup grape juice
>   Juice of 1 lemon
>   1 pint heavy cream
>   1 pound honey

Mix the grape juice and lemon juice. Whip the cream, and add to it, a little at a time, the honey and juices. Place the mixture in the freezer.

Strawberry Ice Cream

>   1 pint strawberries
>   1 cup liquid acacia honey
>   Juice of 3 lemons
>   1 tablespoon vanilla sugar

Place the honey, lemon juice, and sugar in a pan, then bring to a boil. Remove this syrup from the heat and let cool. Quickly wash the strawberries, dry them, remove the stems and purée them. Add the strawberries to the syrup and place this mixture in the freezer. In the same way you can make raspberry ice cream, blueberry ice cream, blackberry ice cream and fig ice cream (the figs must be peeled and the mashed pulp must weigh 1 lb.) .

Fruit Ice Cream

Add one pint heavy cream to the fruit syrup prepared as in the above recipes, freeze.

Cream Ice Cream with Honey Sauce

> 1 cup sugar
> 2 vanilla beans
> ⅓ cup water
> 2 pints heavy cream
> 1 cup of your favorite honey
> ½ pound crushed walnuts

Prepare the syrup by cooking the sugar, water and vanilla beans for twenty minutes, then let cool. Add the cream and freeze. You must be very careful in making this ice cream as it curdles very easily. Sprinkle with the walnuts and serve with a hot honey sauce. (If the honey is too thick add a few tablespoons of water.)

Banana Sauce for Ice Cream

> 6 bananas
> 5 tablespoons acacia or lime honey
> 6 tablespoons milk
> 6 tablespoons rum

Beat all ingredients together, and serve with ice cream.

Lemon Ice Cream

> 1 pint water
> 1½ cups liquid acacia honey
> 1 vanilla bean
> 5 large lemons

Place the water, honey and vanilla bean in a pan, boil for 10 minutes over low heat, then let cool. Grate the peel of the lemons (only the yellow part, as the white part is bitter) , and add to the honey syrup. Wait 2 hours then add the juice of the lemons and leave for another ½ hour. Strain this syrup and freeze.

Orange Ice Cream

> 1 pint water
> 1½ cups orange honey
> 1 vanilla bean
> 4 oranges
> Juice of 1 lemon

Prepare as Lemon Ice Cream.

Grapefruit Ice Cream

  1 pint water
  1½ cups acacia honey
  1 vanilla bean
  2 large grapefruits
  Juice of 1 lemon

Prepare as Lemon Ice Cream.

Chocolate Ice Cream

  2 pints milk
  1 cup acacia or orange honey
  8 egg yolks
  10 ounces bitter chocolate
  3 tablespoons cocoa

Beat the milk, cocoa and honey, pour in a pan and bring to a boil. Beat the egg yolks until foamy. Melt the chocolate in a double boiler and pour together with the milk over the egg yolks. Place the mixture in a double boiler, and bring to a boil. Remove from flame, let cool and freeze.

Tangerine Ice Cream

  1 pint water
  1½ cups acacia honey
  1 vanilla bean
  5 tangerines
  Juice of 1 lemon

Prepare as Lemon Ice Cream.

Pineapple Ice Cream

  1 pint water
  1½ cups acacia honey
  1 cinnamon stick
  1 medium pineapple
  Juice of 1 lemon

Peel the pineapple, remove the hard center and juice the pulp. Proceed as in Lemon Ice Cream.

JAMS

You can make very good jams using honey. Certainly they will be more healthful than the ones made with white sugar. It is necessary, though, to follow a few essential rules:

Always use light or amber colored honey such as the ones from acacia and eucalyptus, and if possible use a liquid honey.

The fruit must always be very ripe, unless otherwise specified. The proportions are always the same: 2 cups honey to 1 lb. of fruit.

Always soak the fruit in the liquid (or melted) honey for twenty-four hours before cooking it. Do not soak it in a metal container, and mix occasionally to avoid a honey deposit at the bottom.

The cooking time varies from fifteen to forty-five minutes, depending on the type of fruit, the jam will be ready when a drop fallen on a dish and cooled, will not slide if the dish is tilted.

Place the jams in jars when cooled, cover with wax paper dipped in alcohol, and seal.

Plum Jam

Peel the plums and cut in half before soaking them in the honey.

Blueberry Jam

Rinse the blueberries, quickly drain well and press lightly with a fork before soaking in the honey, this way they will blend better.

Apricot Jam

Choose some soft and well ripened apricots, cut in thin slices so that the honey will be completely absorbed.

Peach Jam

Peel the peaches (if the skin is hard to remove, dip them for a few minutes in boiling water), and cut in thin slices. This jam will have to cook longer as peaches contain less sugar than other fruit.

Fig Jam

Choose well ripened and soft figs. Remove the stem and skin. Don't cook any longer than twenty minutes.

Prune Jam

Dried pitted prunes are used. It is a jam made in the winter when there is no fresh fruit available. Make some holes in the prunes using a fork. Soak in water for twelve hours, then boil over high heat in a lot of water for a few minutes. Drain and mash. Place the same quantity of honey in a pan, with some water (1/4 cup for each cup of honey). Boil for ten minutes, skim, add the prunes and cook for thirty minutes.

Grape Jam

Choose some sweet grapes, with not too thick a skin. Wash well, drain, remove from stems, weigh, then flatten with a fork before soaking in the honey. Cook this jam for a little longer then the other jams: about forty-five minutes.

Chestnut Jam

Remove the hard skin from the chestnuts, boil for a few minutes, then remove the thinner skin. Cook in water until tender, then mash them. For each pound of chestnuts, add 2 cups of honey and 1/2 cup water. Mix well and soak for twenty-four hours. Add a vanilla bean and cook for fifteen to twenty minutes.

Pumpkin Jam

Peel a pumpkin, cut the pulp in small cubes, and boil for ten minutes. Drain and cool. Add 2 cups honey for each pound of raw pumpkin. Soak for twenty-four hours, then cook for twenty minutes with a vanilla bean.

Orange and Honey Jam (recipe from L'angolo della Gastronomia)

3⅓ pounds oranges
2 pounds honey
1 pound orange peel

Boil the orange peel in a lot of water for two hours. Drain and weigh: it should weigh about two-thirds of a pound. Cut into thin strips. Squeeze the oranges, to obtain two pints juice. Mix the juice, peels and honey, and cook for about thirty minutes. Test for readiness by placing a spoonful on a dish, it must be thick when cooled. When the jam has cooled pour it in the jars, seal with wax paper dipped in pure alcohol.

Carrot Jam

Clean the carrots, cut into thin strips and boil for twenty minutes. Drain. Let cool, and add 2 cups honey for every 1 lb. of carrots. Soak for twenty-four hours then cook for twenty minutes with a vanilla bean.

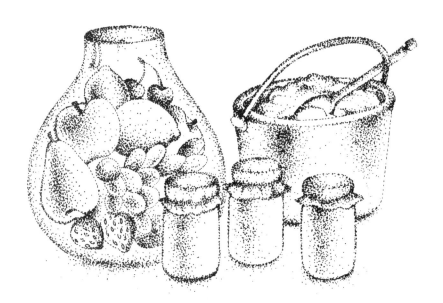